Nicola Graimes is an experienced health, cookery and food writer. She is the author of over 20 books and winner of the Best Vegetarian Cookbook in the UK in the World Gourmand Awards 2002, and Best Family Cookbook in the UK in the World Gourmand Awards 2004, as well as a finalist in the Le Cordon Bleu World Media Awards in 2007.

By the Same Author

QUICK & EASY
LOW-FAT RECIPES

LOSE WEIGHT – FEEL GREAT

NICOLA GRAIMES

WATKINS PUBLISHING

LONDON

This edition published in the UK in 2010 by
Watkins Publishing, Sixth Floor, Castle House,
75–76 Wells Street, London W1T 3QH

1 3 5 7 9 10 8 6 4 2

Designed and typeset by Jerry Goldie Graphic Design

Printed and bound in Great Britain

British Library Cataloguing-in-Publication Data Available

ISBN: 978-1-906787-75-2

www.watkinspublishing.co.uk

Publisher's note: While every care has been taken in compiling the recipes for this book, Watkins Publishers, or any other persons who have been involved in working on this publication, cannot accept responsibility for any errors or omissions, inadvertent or not, that may be found in the recipes or text, or for any problems that may arise as a result of preparing one of these recipes. If you are pregnant or breastfeeding or have any special dietary requirements or medical conditions, it is advisable to consult a medical professional before following any of the recipes contained in this book. Ill or elderly people, babies, young children and women who are pregnant or breastfeeding should avoid any recipes containing uncooked egg whites.

Contents

FOOD WARNING SYMBOLS

If you or a member of your family is vegetarian or has an allergy to or intolerance of nuts, eggs, seeds, gluten, wheat or dairy products, you will find these symbols, which accompany each recipe, invaluable.

(V) vegetarian

(⊘) contains nuts

(O) contains eggs

(⊘) contains seeds

(⊘) contains gluten

(⊛) contains wheat

(⊜) contains dairy

In addition, the menu plans on pages 244–47 give ideas for a week's worth of meals for wheat- and gluten-free, vegetarian, vegan and nut-free diets.

Notes on the recipes

Please note that metric and imperial measurements are given for the recipes. Follow one set of measures only, not a mixture, as they are not interchangeable.

• 1 tsp = 5ml • 1 tbsp = 15ml • 1 cup = 250ml

Unless otherwise stated:
• Use medium eggs
• Use medium fruit and vegetables
• Use fresh herbs

About This Book

We all need fat in our diet. Alongside the many positives that certain types of dietary fat contribute to our health, there's no denying the fact that it also makes food taste good by adding to its flavour, texture and palatability. Fat serves as a carrier for the absorption of fat-soluble vitamins A, D, E and K, and also provides the valuable omega-3 and omega-6 essential fatty acids. Furthermore, it insulates the body and protects some of our internal organs.

Unfortunately, there are also negatives associated with some types of dietary fat. On average, most of us eat around 20 per cent too much saturated fat every day, and this is despite the overwhelming evidence that eating too much saturated fat increases the risk of cardiovascular disease, diabetes, strokes and some forms of cancer, not forgetting weight gain. There is nothing new about this evidence, yet the message still does not appear to be filtering through.

Recent research by the UK's Food Standards Agency confirms that there is still a lot of public confusion about fat, with nearly half of us not fully recognizing that saturated fat is bad for our health, and one in seven people not realizing that reducing intake of saturated fat diminishes the risk of developing coronary heart disease. Also, there is more confusion when it comes to differentiating between those fats that are 'bad' for us and those that are 'good'.

Quick & Easy Low-Fat Recipes aims to redress the balance with its simple, informative guidelines and tips, supported by over 130 nutritious and delicious recipes. Healthy eating and losing weight are not about cutting out fat altogether. In fact, studies have found that extremely low-fat diets are difficult to stick to in the long term, leading to irregular patterns of weight loss and gain. Crucially, it's not just about the amount of fat you eat but also about the types of fat.

This is not a diet book; rather it shows you how to make lifetime changes in the way you eat, leading to long-term good health and a steady pattern of weight loss and maintenance. It may be a cliché, but it's all about eating a varied balance of foods and avoiding those that are processed, which tend to be high in fat, sugar and salt.

READING FOOD LABELS

Most food labels detail the weight of fat, whilst others go one step further, giving separate figures for saturated, monounsaturated and polyunsaturated fats. Some manufacturers in the UK have adopted the traffic-light system, with red indicating a high-fat product, orange medium-fat and green low-fat. However, despite government regulations, labelling on low-fat foods remains confusing, with a range of different terminologies used. Opposite are some of the common terms that are used, plus what they mean.

FAT FIGURES

Fat contains 9 calories per gram (kcal/g) – that's more than double the energy of carbohydrates (4kcal/g) and proteins (3.75kcal/g). Since fats are less bulky (hence less filling) than other food groups, it's also all too easy to over-indulge in them.

The recommended total fat intake is 20–35 per cent of daily calories for adults. In practical terms this means:

WOMEN 2,000 kcals/day – total fat intake/day 50g–70g (1¾–2½oz)

SLIMMING DIET 1,500 kcals/day – total fat intake/day 40–50g (1½–1¾oz)

MEN 2,500 kcals/day – total fat intake/day 70g–90g (2½–3¼oz)

Meanwhile, for children under 3, a total fat intake of 30–35 per cent is recommended, and for those up to 18 years, it's 25–35 per cent.

COMMON TERMS AND THEIR MEANING

TERM	MEANING
High fat	More than 20g/^{3}/$_4$oz fat per 100g/3^1/$_2$oz
High saturated fat	More than 5g/^{1}/$_6$oz saturated fat per 100g/3^1/$_2$oz
Low fat	Less than 3g/^{1}/$_{10}$oz fat per 100g/3^1/$_2$oz
Low saturated fat	Less than 1.5g/^{1}/$_{20}$oz saturated fat per 100g/3^1/$_2$oz
Lean (applies to meat and poultry)	Less than 10g/^{1}/$_3$oz fat per 100g/3^1/$_2$oz and less than 4.5g/^{1}/$_6$oz saturated fat per 100g/3^1/$_2$oz
Extra lean (applies to meat and poultry)	Less than 5g/^{1}/$_8$oz fat per 100g/3^1/$_2$oz and less than 2g/^{1}/$_{16}$oz, saturated fat per 100g/3^1/$_2$oz
Fat free	Less than 0.5g fat per serving
Reduced fat	25% less fat than the food it is being compared to
Light/lite	50% less fat than the regular product
Low cholesterol	20mg or less per serving
Low calorie	40 calories or fewer per serving

What about saturated fat?

Nutritional guidelines recommend that saturated fat makes up no more than 10 per cent of daily calories, and that we limit consumption to a maximum intake of 20g/¾oz a day (women) and 30g/1oz (men).

CHOLESTEROL AND LIPOPROTEINS

In addition to fats, there are also cholesterol and lipoproteins. Cholesterol is a waxy substance that circulates in the blood and forms part of the outer membrane that surrounds every cell. Cholesterol is not all bad: it is essential for our bodies to work, playing a valuable role in the production of some hormones, contributing to the manufacture of bile acids and insulating the nerves, so helping them to work efficiently.

Cholesterol is made naturally in the body and is also found in certain foods, in particular egg yolks, offal and shellfish. Dietary cholesterol was once thought to have a significant effect on cholesterol levels in the body, but its contribution has since been played down, with saturated fat now to blame for harmful increased levels. Once inside the body, the liver turns saturated fat into cholesterol.

Lipoproteins are small molecules whose job it is to circulate cholesterol around the body. There are two main types:

Low-density lipoproteins (LDL) are the harmful or 'bad' cholesterol, since high levels can increase the risk of heart disease.

High-density lipoproteins (HDL) are the protective or 'good' cholesterol, since high levels reduce the risk of heart disease.

TRIGLYCERIDES

These are another type of fatty substance that is found in the blood. People who are overweight, who eat a lot of fatty foods, including dairy, and sugary foods, or who drink too much alcohol are more likely to have a high triglyceride level. This also increases the risk of heart disease.

GOOD FATS, BAD FATS

Dietary fat comes from both plant and animal sources, of which there are three main types: saturated, monounsaturated and polyunsaturated. Most foods contain a mixture of all three but are usually higher in one type than the others, rather than containing an equal balance of all three. There are also trans fats.

Saturated Fat

Generally considered 'bad', saturated fat usually comes from animal sources (apart from coconut and palm oil) and is solid at room temperature. Foods that are high in saturated fat are:

- Coconut oil, coconut cream and palm oil
- Butter, ghee and lard
- Cheese, particularly hard cheese
- Fatty cuts of meat and processed meat products, such as pâtés, sausages and pies
- Pastry
- Cakes and biscuits/cookies
- Some sweets/candy
- Chocolate
- Cream, sour cream, crème fraîche and ice cream
- Some savoury snacks

Saturated fat increases the amount of LDL (harmful cholesterol) and triglycerides in the blood, and has been linked to an increased risk of some of the major killers in the Western world, including coronary heart disease and some cancers. For these reasons, it's a good idea to cut down on the amount of saturated fat we eat.

However, there is growing evidence that a small amount of saturated fat is essential for health and longevity, supporting the immune system.

Unsaturated Fats

Unsaturated fats are split into monounsaturated (MUFA) and polyunsaturated (PUFA) fats and each should provide about one-third of our fat intake.

Monunsaturated Fat

A diet rich in MUFAs (found in plant oils, nuts, seeds and avocados) helps to reduce levels of LDL (unhealthy cholesterol – the type that furs up the arteries) without lowering levels of HDL (healthy cholesterol). Consequently, these fats reduce the risk of heart disease. The American Nurses' Health Study found that for every 5 per cent of saturated fat swapped for monounsaturated fat, the risk of heart disease was reduced by 42 per cent. There is also evidence to suggest that MUFAs might trigger weight loss, even if calories are not reduced. Researchers are not exactly sure how this happens, but suggest that MUFAs speed up the metabolic rate, or encourage the breakdown of fat cells in the body.

Polyunsaturated Fat

Like MUFAs, PUFAs (polyunsaturated fats) help to reduce LDL (harmful cholesterol). They provide the essential fatty acids omega-3 and omega-6, which cannot be made in the body in sufficient amounts and have to be supplied by dietary means.

Omega-3 fats

The health benefits of omega-3 fats are well documented. They help regulate blood pressure, the immune system and blood clotting and have been shown to be essential for the health and development of the nerves, spinal cord, eyes, skin and brain. As for the heart, omega-3 fats have been shown to make the blood less sticky, thereby reducing the risk of both heart attacks and strokes. They also play an anti-inflammatory role, helping people with arthritis.

Good sources of omega-3 are:

Fish sources
- Tuna (fresh)
- Salmon
- Mackerel
- Pilchards
- Herring
- Dogfish
- Trout
- Prawns/shrimp
- Crab

Non-fish sources
- Walnuts and almonds
- Linseeds
- Pumpkin seeds
- Eggs
- Soya beans
- Wheatgerm

According to The British Dietetic Association, to benefit from omega-3, adults and children over 12 are advised to eat two portions of fish per week (a portion is about 140g/5oz cooked), one of which should be oily. This is equal to about 450mg EPA/DHA (long-chain omega-3 fatty acids and the most nutritionally beneficial) per day. Younger children need to eat proportionally less, depending on their age:

- $1\frac{1}{2}$–3 years: one-third of a portion
- 4–6 years: half a portion
- 7–11 years: two-thirds of a portion

Omega-6 fats

These fats are found in nuts, seeds and vegetable oils, such as sunflower, safflower and corn oil. They are essential for growth, cell structure and a healthy immune system, yet generally we have too much omega-6 in our diets as opposed to omega-3, and this can lead to its own health problems if not eaten in balance. The optimal ratio of omega-6 to omega-3 is thought to be 4:1 or lower.

Trans Fats

Most trans fats are vegetable oils that have been chemically altered or hydrogenated – a process that turns them into solid or semi-solid fats (think margarines and spreads). Over the last few years, trans fats have been the focus of much negative publicity (and rightly so). Consequently, many food manufacturers have reduced their usage of trans fats, but do check the ingredients lists on food products such as pies, biscuits/cookies, cakes, fried foods and pastry for hydrogenated fats/oils. Note that the higher up the list trans fats appear, the more the food is likely to contain. Trans fats also occur naturally in small amounts in dairy products, beef and lamb, and products made from these foods.

The problem with trans fats is that, like saturated fat, they raise levels of LDL ('bad' cholesterol) as well as triglycerides. However, unlike saturated fat, trans fats also reduce levels of HDL ('good' cholesterol) – making them potentially worse for our health than saturated fat.

SWITCHING TO A LOW-FAT DIET

There are a number of very simple steps you can adopt to reduce the amount of saturated fat you eat. However, it is also important to keep an eye on your total fat intake, as too much is not good for health and eventually leads to weight gain. For ease of reference, foods are split into their main groups:

Dairy

The foods in this group are a good source of protein, vitamins and minerals, particularly calcium and magnesium, which are essential for healthy bones and teeth. Contrary to popular belief, reducing the fat content in dairy foods does not lower calcium levels, in fact you get slightly more of the mineral in skimmed milk than in whole or semi-skimmed/reduced-fat milk.

- Switching to low-fat dairy products couldn't be easier, with so many alternatives now available, including reduced-fat versions of cream, crème fraîche, sour cream, cheese, yogurt and milk. However, choose sensibly – even though it says 'reduced-fat' on the label, these foods can still contain a fair amount of fat.

- Opt for soft cheeses, which are naturally lower in fat than hard cheeses, such as mozzarella (there is also a light version available) or ricotta. If you need a strong-flavoured hard cheese, either opt for reduced-fat versions or choose a mature vintage variety (of which only a small amount will be needed to add flavour to a dish). Using 50g/1¾oz low-fat cheese rather than 50g/1¾oz ordinary cheese saves about 5g/⅛oz saturated fat, while using 25g/1oz strong-tasting cheese rather than 50g/1¾oz milder cheese will achieve roughly the same 5g/⅛oz saving in saturated fat.

- There are also some simple steps that can help, including: grating cheese rather than slicing it to help you eat less; cutting the rind off 'bloomy' cheeses such as Brie and Camembert to reduce the fat content by around half; and going easy on creamy sauces: opt instead for tomato-based ones, or choose lemon juice and herbs to add flavour instead.

Meat and Poultry

The foods in this group are valuable sources of vitamins, minerals and protein, but since meat and meat products are a also major source of saturated fat, it is a good idea to wise up to which types are higher in fat than others.

- Poultry is lower in fat than red meat, but only as long as the skin is removed; this can be done after cooking if you want it to stay moist. Also, dark poultry meat contains more fat than white meat.

- Choose lean cuts of meat and poultry and remove visible white fat before cooking. Use lean beef mince or choose turkey mince instead, which is lower in fat. Back bacon is lower in fat than streaky bacon, while lamb and processed meat products, such as sausages, contain the most fat, especially saturated.

- Meat and poultry suit low-fat methods of cooking such as stir-frying, grilling and char-grilling (see Cooking Tips, page 12).

Fish and Shellfish

Low in saturated fat and a good source of protein, seafood can play an important part in a healthy, low-fat diet. It is recommended that we eat two servings a week (a serving is 140g/5oz cooked), one of which should be an oily fish (see pages 7–8).

- While in the past people on low-fat diets have been encouraged to reduce all types of fat, numerous studies highlight that the health benefits of oily fish far outweigh any negatives associated with their fat content – as long as they are not deep-fried!

- Similarly, it used to be advised that shellfish, particularly prawns/shrimp, should be avoided, or at least eaten rarely, due to their high cholesterol content. However, recent studies have shown that dietary cholesterol has little effect on the amount of cholesterol in the body. Indeed, saturates and trans fats have been found to have a greater negative impact on cholesterol levels.

• Seafood, in particular, suits low-fat methods of cooking such as steaming, baking, grilling and griddling or char-grilling.

Oils and Fats

Vegetable oils and olive oil are low in saturated fat and the preferred choice for cooking and making salad dressings.

• Remember that monounsaturated fats, such as olive oil, sesame oil and rapeseed oil, can be damaged by sunlight, so it is best to buy them in dark bottles or store them in a dark cupboard. They should also not be heated too high when cooking, as they oxidize, creating free radicals in the body. Some oils, such as corn or groundnut, are more suited to use at high temperatures.

• Butter tastes great, but it's also high in saturated fat. If using butter, restrict yourself to using minimal amounts, and, if possible, switch to a half-fat variety.

According to the Fat Panel (UK), these are the percentages of saturated fat contained in oils and butter:

Rapeseed oil 8%
Sunflower oil 12%
Corn/maize oil 14%
Olive oil 15%
Soya bean oil 16%
Butter 54%

Fruit and vegetables

The ultimate health food, fruit and vegetables should play a key part of any low-fat diet, providing plentiful amounts of vitamins, minerals and beneficial plant phytochemicals.

- Take care when adding sauces to vegetables or when dressing salads, because such additions can seriously boost the levels of fat. Also avoid adding butter to cooked vegetables. Try making low-fat salad dressings with miso, fruit juice, yogurt, herbs, spices or tomato juice in place of oil, or at least to replace some of it.

- Many snacks can be high in saturated fat and additives, so pick up some fresh fruit, dried fruit or raw vegetable sticks to satisfy hunger pangs instead.

COOKING TIPS

Not surprisingly, frying and deep-frying increase fat levels. If a recipe calls for frying, it is best to use a heavy-based, non-stick frying pan to keep the amount of oil required to a minimum. If the pan becomes dry, add a splash of water, wine or stock to add moisture. As for deep-frying – there is only one response: avoid it.

The following are preferable alternative methods of cooking, but also consider the microwave and baking, which can be useful in the low-fat kitchen.

Stir-frying

When stir-frying, preheat the wok before adding a small amount of oil, which will then seal the ingredients quickly, helping to retain their moisture during cooking . Using a non-stick wok will also allow you to keep any added oil to a minimum; alternatively, use stock, Chinese cooking wine or sherry in place of the oil.

Steaming

This is not only an excellent low-fat method of cooking, it also helps to preserve the water-soluble vitamins B and C, which are lost in boiled food. The cooking water can be kept afterwards and used as a base for a stock.

Char-grilling

Little or no fat is needed when char-grilling, or griddling, which is a suitable method of cooking fruit, vegetables, poultry, meat and seafood. What's more, any excess fat drains away from the food into the ridges of the griddle pan. To ensure successful char-grilling, first brush the foods lightly with oil, if using, rather than adding the oil to the pan (you will use less this way). Also, make sure you preheat the griddle to help seal what you are cooking. Instead of using oil, you could marinate foods beforehand, then baste them during cooking to keep them moist.

Grilling

This method also requires little or no fat and gives food a crisp, golden exterior. Use a rack when grilling, especially for meat and poultry, so any fat can drip through rather than puddling around the food. When cooking fish, however, it is fine to line the grill pan with foil to prevent it sticking. Preheat the grill to seal the food quickly and so retain the moisture. As with char-grilling, instead of using oil, you could marinate foods beforehand, then baste during cooking to keep foods moist.

En Papillote

By putting food in a parcel of baking parchment or foil, you can seal in flavour, nutrients and juices, and little or no oil is needed. Bake or steam the parcel, but take care when unwrapping food as the parcels can be very hot and steamy inside.

Poaching

This simple method of cooking meat, poultry, fish and eggs involves immersing them in a hot liquid, such as stock, water or wine, until cooked. The liquid is heated until just bubbling and is kept at a steady tremble rather than a vigorous boil. Poaching can take place on the hob or in the oven, requires no fat and helps to keep foods moist and succulent.

ABOUT THE RECIPES

The recipes in this collection, divided into Breakfasts & Brunches, Light Meals, Main Meals and Desserts, are easy to make and quick to prepare. Many will keep for a few days in the fridge, whilst others can be frozen for future use, allowing you to plan ahead and take the hassle out of mealtimes. Choose from an inspiring range of world flavours from different cuisines as well as low-fat versions of family favourites.

Each recipe comes with a nutritional breakdown, detailing calories, total fat and saturated fat, enabling you to mix-and-match recipes and record the amount of fat eaten on a daily basis, keeping it within the recommended guidelines (see page 2). It also comes with an explanation of its health benefits as well as serving suggestions, enabling you to create nutritionally balanced low-fat meals.

The invaluable Menu Plans on pages 244–7 show how to keep track of your fat intake, enabling you to balance meals on a daily basis, from breakfast through to dinner, so if you choose a higher-fat lunch then opt for a lower-fat dinner. By actively reducing the amount of fat you eat as much as possible, you will be able to enjoy those occasional treats, such as chocolate!

Breakfasts & Brunches

Research by health experts has shown that people who skip breakfast are prone to grab unhealthy snacks mid-morning; and, more often than not, such snacks are likely to be ones that are high in fat, such as crisps, pastries, muffins, cookies and the like.... However, you need to watch out for low-fat snacks, too – because if you eat more than a single serving size, you could be eating far more fat then you think.

It may sound obvious, but by preparing your own meals you have control over what you eat and what goes into your food, and there's no better time to start than with the first meal of the day.

The recipes in this chapter cater for all tastes and requirements, whether you are looking for a quick and healthy bite to eat before you rush off to work, such as the Berry Scrunch (packed with nutritious seeds, oats and fruit), the light, yet sustaining, Almond Banana Shake or the Fruit & Nut Muesli, or whether you need a more substantial savoury dish, such as Smoked Trout Rolls (high in beneficial omega-3 fats), the low-fat, protein-rich Char-grilled Chicken & Pepper Toasts or the Sunday Breakfast Platter: a relaxed, throw-it-together-type of brunch comprising ham, fruit and vegetables served with a creamy herb dip.

Hot Vanilla Chocolate

Raw cacao can be found in health food shops or is widely available online. This warming drink is equally good served chilled.

SERVES 1   **PREPARATION** 5 minutes   **COOKING** 3 minutes

1 tbsp raw cacao powder or drinking chocolate powder

250ml/9fl oz/1 cup 1% fat or skimmed milk

1/4 tsp vanilla extract

1/2 tsp agave syrup

ground cinnamon or nutmeg, to sprinkle (optional)

1   In a mug, mix together the raw cacao powder with a little of the milk to make a paste.

2   Warm the remaining milk in a heavy-based saucepan over a low heat, stir in the vanilla extract and pour into the mug. Stir in agave syrup to sweeten and sprinkle with cinnamon, if using.

Health benefits

The cacao bean (and its by-products powder and nibs) is pure and unadulterated. Cacao, also called raw chocolate, is sugar free and is particularly rich in antioxidants and magnesium, which supports the heart and digestion, helps with PMS and cramps, and, in conjunction with calcium, helps to build strong bones and teeth.

Food Facts per Portion

Calories 145kcal • Total Fat 1.4g • saturated fat 0.8g

Almond Banana Shake

Rich and creamy, this protein-packed smoothie is perfect if you are not a fan of a big breakfast but are looking for something quick and nutritious. Grinding the almonds yourself rather than buying ground almonds gives a more nutty, less powdery texture.

SERVES 2   **PREPARATION** 5 minutes

30g/1oz/scant ¼ cup whole blanched almonds

400ml/14fl oz/1²/₃ cups light soya milk

2 bananas, halved

1 tsp vanilla extract

ground nutmeg, to sprinkle

1 Process the almonds in a blender or food processor until they are finely ground.

2 Add the soya milk, bananas and vanilla extract and blend until smooth and creamy. Pour into two glasses and sprinkle with nutmeg before serving.

Health benefits

Soya products are rich in protein and low in saturated fat and cholesterol. For people suffering from high cholesterol, research shows that including at least 25g/1oz soya protein each day can help to reduce levels of harmful cholesterol when part of a low-fat diet.

Food Facts per Portion

Calories 239kcal • Total Fat 11.9g • saturated fat 1.2g

Strawberry & Ricotta Muffins

Ricotta is a fresh, light cheese, which makes a useful, calcium-rich addition to a low-fat diet. It can be used in both sweet and savoury dishes, and its mild taste means it has a natural affinity with more robust flavours.

SERVES 4   **PREPARATION** 10 minutes   **COOKING** 2 minutes

4 wholemeal muffins

6 tbsp ricotta cheese

2 tbsp agave syrup

1 tsp vanilla extract

2 large handfuls strawberries, hulled and sliced

1 Split the muffins in half crossways and toast lightly on both sides.

2 Meanwhile, put the ricotta, agave syrup and vanilla extract in a bowl and beat lightly with a wooden spoon. Top each muffin half with some of the ricotta mixture and follow with the sliced strawberries, then serve.

Health Benefits

A natural sweetener derived from a cactus in Mexico, agave syrup can be used in place of sugar and other sweeteners, and since it is about 25 per cent sweeter, less is needed. It also provides iron, magnesium, potassium and calcium.

Food Facts per Portion

Calories 194kcal • Total Fat 3.6g • saturated fat 1.8g

Berry Scrunch

Ⓥ ◔ ◑ ◉

Any seasonal fruit can be used instead of the berries, or use drained tinned (in natural juice) or frozen fruit.

SERVES 2   **PREPARATION** 8 minutes   **COOKING** 3 minutes

4 tbsp whole porridge oats

2 tbsp sunflower seeds

handful raspberries or strawberries, hulled and sliced

125g/4$\frac{1}{2}$oz/heaped cup $\frac{1}{2}$ virtually fat-free fromage frais

2 tbsp skimmed milk

2 tsp clear honey

1   Put the oats and sunflower seeds in a frying pan and dry-fry over a medium heat, stirring regularly, for 2–3 minutes until light golden, taking care because the seeds can burn easily.

2   Divide the berries between two bowls. Add the fromage frais and milk, then mix gently together. Sprinkle with the toasted oats and seeds, then drizzle with honey before serving.

Health Benefits

Whole oats are absorbed by the body quite slowly, thereby avoiding unwanted peaks and troughs in blood-sugar levels and enabling you to feel full for longer. Oats also contain essential fatty acids and are a good source of vitamins E, B1 and B2.

Food Facts per Portion

Calories 270kcal • Total Fat 9.9g • saturated fat 1.2g

Winter Fruit Compote

The cinnamon, star anise and cloves add a wonderful warmth to this fibre-rich dried fruit salad. If preferred, the fruit can be puréed after cooking to make a naturally sweet topping for porridge/oatmeal or muesli.

SERVES 4   **PREPARATION** 5 minutes   **COOKING** 10–15 minutes

300g/10½oz/scant 2 cups mixed dried fruit, such as figs, pears, apricots and prunes

300ml/10½fl oz/1¼ cups fresh orange juice

2 cinnamon sticks

1 star anise

3 cloves

4 heaped tbsp low-fat fromage frais, to serve (optional)

1   Put all the ingredients in a saucepan with 185ml/6fl oz/¾ cup water. Bring to the boil, then reduce the heat and simmer, covered, for 10–15 minutes until the fruit has softened.

2   Remove from the heat and leave to cool slightly before dividing between four bowls. Serve with a spoonful of fromage frais, if liked.

Storage

Can be stored in an airtight container in the refrigerator for up to 3 days.

Health Benefits

Fibre is found in significant amounts in dried fruit, which protects against constipation and can help with weight management because it helps us to feel full for longer. Dried fruit also has a higher concentration of some vitamins and minerals, particularly iron, than its fresh counterparts, but nevertheless should be eaten in moderate amounts due to its high sugar content.

Food Facts per Portion

Calories 174kcal • Total Fat 0.7g • saturated fat 0g

Fresh Fruit Compote with Yogurt

After tasting this indulgently creamy and fruity confection, it may come as a surprise to you to discover that it is low in fat. Make sure the berries and nectarines are perfectly ripe for the best flavour. Alternatively, if they are out of season, you could use drained tinned fruit in natural juice.

SERVES 4   **PREPARATION** 10 minutes

225g/8oz/1⅓ cups raspberries or strawberries, hulled and halved if necessary

4 nectarines, pitted and roughly chopped

200g/7oz/scant 1 cup 0% fat Greek yogurt

150ml/5fl oz/scant ⅔ cup low-fat natural bio yogurt

2 tbsp toasted flaked almonds, to serve (optional)

1   Set aside 4 raspberries or strawberries. Put the remaining berries in a blender or food processor with the nectarines and blend until puréed. Press the purée through a sieve to remove the seeds, if preferred. Divide the purée between four glasses.

2   Mix together the Greek yogurt and bio yogurt and spoon over the top of the fruit purée.

3   Scatter over the almonds, if using, then top with the reserved fruit before serving.

Storage

The fruit purée can be stored in an airtight container in the refrigerator for up to 3 days.

Health benefits

Rich in vitamin C, raspberries are an excellent source of valuable antioxidants that work together to protect against the risks of certain cancers, heart disease and age-relative cognitive decline.

Food Facts per Portion (with almonds)

Calories 160kcal • Total Fat 4.9g • saturated fat 0.7g

Fruit & Nut Muesli

Ⓥ Ⓞ Ⓓ Ⓖ ⓐ

This healthy muesli contains a nutritious mix of nuts and seeds, providing beneficial polyunsaturated fats known to reduce harmful cholesterol in the body. Try varying the selection according to what you have to hand.

SERVES 4 **PREPARATION** 10 minutes

8 ready-to-eat dates, roughly chopped

4 tbsp sunflower seeds

2 tbsp flaked almonds

50g/1³/₄oz/heaped ¼ cup walnuts, roughly chopped

60g/2oz/½ cup whole porridge oats

2 sweet apples

250g/9oz/heaped 1 cup 0% fat Greek yogurt

125ml/4fl oz/½ cup skimmed milk, to serve

1 Mix together the dates, seeds, nuts and oats in a bowl and divide between four breakfast bowls.

2 Grate the apples, still with their skins on, and discarding the cores, then divide the grated apple between the bowls.

3 Share the yogurt and milk between each serving, then stir until combined. Serve.

Storage

The dry ingredients can be kept in an airtight container for up to 5 days.

Health Benefits

The almond is one of the most nutritious nuts around, being rich in protein and providing beneficial unsaturated fats, which may help to reduce levels of harmful cholesterol in the body. Vitamin E, magnesium and potassium are also present in beneficial amounts.

Food Facts per Portion

Calories 347kcal • Total Fat 21.5g • saturated fat 2.4g

Variations

Brazil nuts, cashews, pecans or hazelnuts would all make suitable alternatives to the walnuts. You could also try a mixture of berries, sliced banana or nectarines in place of the apples.

Banana Porridge/Oatmeal

Full of valuable fibre, vitamins and minerals, porridge/oatmeal is wonderfully comforting and makes a sustaining start to the day. The sliced banana adds natural sweetness. Milk alternatives such as soya or oat can also be used, but you could also use other types of fruit, including berries, chopped apple, raisins or dates.

SERVES 4   **PREPARATION** 5 minutes   **COOKING** 15 minutes

200g/7oz/scant 2 cups whole porridge oats

750ml/26fl oz/3 cups skimmed milk

2 small bananas, sliced

4 tbsp 0% fat Greek yogurt

2 tbsp chopped walnuts or favourite nuts

4 tsp agave syrup or honey (optional)

1 Put the oats in a pan with the milk and 600ml/21fl oz/scant 2½ cups water. Bring to the boil, then reduce the heat and simmer over a very low heat, half-covered, for 8–10 minutes, stirring frequently.

2 To serve, divide the porridge/oatmeal between four bowls and top with the sliced bananas, a spoonful of the Greek yogurt and a sprinkling of walnuts. Drizzle with agave syrup, if using, then serve.

Health Benefits

Numerous studies highlight the health benefits of walnuts, and this humble nut is one of the richest non-fish sources of omega-3 fatty acids. This essential nutrient has to be supplied by the diet and provides a whole host of health benefits, including protection of the heart, brain and eyes and helping conditions such as arthritis, asthma and eczema.

Food Facts per Portion

Calories 361kcal • Total Fat 9.2g • saturated fat 0.9g

Roast Mushrooms with Bacon on Muffins

Mushrooms readily soak up oil when fried, but when roasted in a foil parcel they cook in their own steam, which helps to retain moisture and reduces the amount of fat required. To keep fat levels down in this recipe, choose lean back/Canadian bacon and grill rather than fry it. The muffins will soak up the delicious mushroom juices.

SERVES 4   **PREPARATION** 10 minutes   **COOKING** 25 minutes

---

4 large portobello mushrooms, stalks removed and wiped of any dirt

1 tsp olive oil

juice of ½ small lemon

4 lean back/Canadian bacon rashers, fat removed

2 wholemeal muffins

2 tbsp quark

1 tsp creamed horseradish

1 tbsp snipped fresh chives

salt and freshly ground black pepper

1   Preheat the oven to 200°C/400°F/Gas 6. Put the mushrooms on a piece of foil large enough to make a parcel. Drizzle over the olive oil, squeeze over the lemon juice and season. Fold up the foil to encase the mushrooms and put the parcel on a baking sheet. Cook the mushrooms in the preheated oven for 20 minutes or until tender.

2   If you have a combined oven/grill, switch the oven to the grill
setting and leave the mushrooms in the oven to keep warm
while you grill the bacon until crisp; alternatively, cook the
bacon under a separate preheated grill. Halve the muffins
crossways and slip under the grill with the bacon, and toast on
both sides. While the bacon and muffins are grilling, mix
together the quark and horseradish. Remove the bacon and
muffins from the grill.

3   Remove the mushrooms from the oven and place a mushroom
on top of each toasted muffin half, then drizzle over the juices.
Top with a spoonful of the quark mixture and a rasher of bacon.
Sprinkle with chives and season to taste before serving.

Health Benefits

Mushrooms are a good source of the mineral potassium. Essential
for controlling the balance of fluids in the body, potassium also
helps to reduce high blood pressure and the linked risk of a stroke.

Food Facts per Portion

Calories 120kcal • Total Fat 3.3g • saturated fat 0.9g

Sunday Breakfast Platter

This is a relaxed 'throw-it-together' type of breakfast, which would also make a perfect informal weekend brunch. Quantities can easily be altered according to the number of people you are feeding and what you have to hand.

SERVES 4   **PREPARATION** 15 minutes   **COOKING** 2 minutes

4 slices lean ham

8 chicory leaves

2 apples, halved, cored and sliced

4 large vine-ripened tomatoes, cut into wedges

4 slices light rye bread

Quark & herb dip:

115g/4oz/$\frac{1}{2}$ cup quark

3 tbsp chopped fresh flat-leaf parsley

3 tbsp chopped fresh basil

1 tbsp fresh lemon juice

salt and freshly ground black pepper

1   Put all the ingredients for the quark and herb dip in a bowl and beat together with a wooden spoon. Transfer the dip to a small serving bowl.

2   Arrange the ham, chicory leaves, apples and tomatoes on a serving plate.

3   Lightly toast the rye bread on both sides, then cut the slices
    in half and add to the serving plate. Serve with the quark and
    herb dip.

Health Benefits

Quark is a spreadable German soft cheese that makes a great low-fat alternative to cream cheese, sour cream or crème fraîche, yet still provides beneficial amounts of calcium, which is good for the bones and teeth.

Food Facts per Portion

Calories 140kcal • Total Fat 1.5g • saturated fat 0.4g

Breakfast Frittata

O

This Italian flat omelette is similar to a Spanish tortilla and is best served warm cut into wedges, accompanied by crusty wholemeal bread. Grilled rashers of lean bacon or pancetta can be swapped for the ham. You could also add a scattering of oregano or basil.

SERVES 4   **PREPARATION** 10 minutes   **COOKING** 15 minutes

2 tsp rapeseed oil

1 large onion, sliced

2 lean slices thickly cut smoked ham, diced

10 small plum tomatoes, halved

4 eggs, lightly beaten

salt and freshly ground black pepper

1   Heat the oil in a medium non-stick frying pan with a heatproof handle. Fry the onion for 8 minutes, stirring regularly, until softened but not browned (add a splash of water if the onion appears too dry).

2   Preheat the grill to medium-high. Add the ham and tomatoes to the onion and smooth into an even layer. Season the eggs and pour them over the top. Cook for 3 minutes without stirring the omelette.

3   Put the pan under the preheated grill for a further 3 minutes until the top is just cooked. Remove from the pan and serve cut into wedges.

Storage

Can be stored in an airtight container in the refrigerator for up to 2 days. Serve cold or wrap in foil and reheat in the oven.

Health Benefits

Rapeseed oil is rich in both omega-6 and omega-3 fatty acids in a 2:1 ratio. It is said to be one of the most heart-friendly oils due to its ability to reduce cholesterol levels, and is also rich in vitamin E. In addition, rapeseed oil has a high smoking point, which means that it is more stable when heated than some other oils, such as olive oil. Choose cold-pressed oil if possible, as it is less refined.

Food Facts per Portion

Calories 137kcal • Total Fat 8.4g • saturated fat 2.1g

Char-grilled Chicken & Pepper Toasts

Char-grilling is an excellent way of adding flavour to food without the need for excessive amounts of oil. Rule number one is to preheat the griddle pan first, which will ensure you get those lovely seared marks and slightly barbecued flavour. It will also help to seal whatever you are cooking and keep it moist inside. Rule number two is to brush the food, rather than the griddle pan itself, with oil.

SERVES 4   **PREPARATION** 10 minutes   **COOKING** 15 minutes

2 skinless chicken breasts, about 175g/6oz each, cut into strips

1 red bell pepper, deseeded and cut into strips

1 yellow bell pepper, deseeded and cut into strips

1 tsp olive oil

2 onion bagels

2 tbsp half-fat humous

squeeze of lemon juice

handful torn fresh basil, to scatter

salt and freshly ground black pepper

1 Preheat a griddle pan. Lightly brush the chicken and pepper strips with the oil. Char-grill the chicken in the griddle pan for 6–8 minutes, turning once, or until cooked through, then set aside. Meanwhile, char-grill the bell peppers for about 6 minutes until slightly blackened around the edges.

2 Split the bagels in half crossways and lightly toast on both
sides, then spread with the humous. Arrange the chicken and
pepper strips on top and squeeze over the lemon juice. Season
to taste and scatter with the basil before serving.

Health Benefits

Humous makes a good substitute for butter, spread on toast or in
sandwiches, and has a fraction of the fat content, especially the
low-fat variety. Made from chickpeas/garbanzo beans, humous is
a good source of soluble fibre, B vitamins, iron, folic acid and other
minerals. Studies show that people who eat pulses on a regular
basis can lower their cholesterol levels by almost 20 per cent, which
has been attributed to the high fibre content.

Food Facts per Portion

Calories 260kcal • Total Fat 4.2g • saturated fat 0.6g

Smoked Trout Rolls

A simple version of sushi rolls, these make an elegant breakfast-cum-brunch, suitable for a weekend treat, when served with slices of wholemeal bread and lemon wedges for squeezing over. Choose cured smoked trout, rather than cooked.

SERVES 4   **PREPARATION** 15 minutes

225g/8oz smoked trout, cut into 12 x 4cm/1½in strips

4 tbsp low-fat soft cheese

1 small cucumber, deseeded and cut into matchsticks

2 tbsp snipped fresh chives

2 tbsp lemon juice, plus wedges to serve (optional)

freshly ground black pepper

12 long chives, to tie the rolls (optional)

1   Lay out the strips of trout on a chopping board. Put a small spoonful of cream cheese at one end of each strip, then put 2 sticks of cucumber crossways on top. Sprinkle with chives.

2   Squeeze over the lemon juice, season with pepper and roll up each strip of trout into a roll.

3   Tie a chive around each roll, if using, and serve with lemon wedges for squeezing over, if liked.

Storage

Can be stored in an airtight container in the refrigerator for up to 1 day.

Health Benefits

Trout is part of the oily fish family and as such is rich in beneficial omega-3 fatty acids. These are found to benefit the brain, skin and eyes and to aid metabolism. The protective effects of fish oils are said to develop within 4 weeks of increasing consumption and if eaten on a regular basis.

Food Facts per Portion

Calories 101kcal • Total Fat 4.3g • saturated fat 1.4g

Kedgeree

This classic rice and smoked fish dish contains the perfect combination of unrefined carbohydrates and low-fat protein.

SERVES 4   **PREPARATION** 10 minutes   **COOKING** 35–40 minutes

250g/9oz/1⅓ cups brown basmati rice, rinsed

2 bay leaves

4 cardamom pods, split

2 tsp bouillon powder

1 tbsp sunflower oil

1 large onion, chopped

2 tbsp garam masala

2 tsp turmeric

juice of ½ lemon

250g/9oz each cod and undyed smoked haddock fillets
    or 250g/9oz each haddock and undyed cod fillets

chopped fresh coriander/cilantro, to scatter

salt and freshly ground black pepper

1 Put the rice in a saucepan and pour cold water over to cover it by 1cm (½ in). Add the bay leaves, cardamom pods and bouillon powder. Bring to the boil, then cover the pan with a tight-fitting lid and reduce the heat to the lowest possible setting.

2 Cook the rice, without removing the lid, for 25–30 minutes until the water is absorbed and the grains are tender. Taste the

rice and, if it is cooked, replace the lid, remove the pan from the heat and leave to stand for 5 minutes. If the rice is still a little hard, add a touch more hot water, replace the lid and return to the heat for another 5 minutes before testing again.

3 Meanwhile, heat the oil in a large frying pan and cook the onion for about 8 minutes until tender and beginning to brown. Stir in the ground spices and cook for 1 minute. Add the lemon juice.

4 While the rice and onion are cooking, put the fish in a large sauté pan and cover with water. Bring the water to a simmer and cook the fish, occasionally spooning the water over it, for about 5 minutes, or until just cooked and opaque.

5 Remove the fish from the pan with a fish slice and put it on a plate, then remove the skin and any bones. Break the fish into large chunks and add to the rice with the spicy onions. Turn to coat and heat through. Season to taste and divide the mixture between four bowls. Scatter with coriander/cilantro, then serve.

Health Benefits

Brown rice is both sustaining and nutritious and, unlike white rice, which is more refined, it produces a more gentle rise in blood sugar, avoiding the unsettling peaks and troughs that have been linked to increased free radical damage in the body and an increased risk of cardiovascular disease.

Food Facts per Portion

Calories 395kcal • Total Fat 6.6g • saturated fat 0.9g

Smoked Fish & Spinach

Try to buy MSC (Marine Stewardship Council) labelled haddock where possible. The label acknowledges and rewards sustainable fishing practices and helps to protect the marine environment. If possible, avoid the artificially coloured bright yellow smoked fillets.

SERVES 4   **PREPARATION** 20 minutes   **COOKING** 5 minutes

500g/1lb 2oz smoked fish, such as haddock (preferably undyed)

500g/1lb 2oz/5½ cups spinach, tough stalks removed, rinsed well

2 wholemeal bagels

4 tsp lemon juice

2 tsp half-fat crème fraîche

2 tsp tartare sauce

freshly ground black pepper

1   Put the smoked fish in a large sauté pan – you may need to cut the fillet in half crossways to enable it to fit in. Cover with boiling water (taking care not to splash yourself) and poach the fish for 3–5 minutes, covered, until cooked, depending on the thickness of the fillet.

2   Meanwhile, steam the spinach for 3 minutes until wilted and softened. Drain well, removing any excess water.

3   Preheat the grill to medium. Remove the fish from the pan using a fish slice and put it on a plate, then peel off the skin, remove any bones and cut the fillet into 4 portions.

4   Split the bagels crossways and toast lightly. Place half a toasted bagel on each plate, top with the spinach and haddock then squeeze the lemon juice over. Season with pepper.

5   Mix together the crème fraîche and tartare sauce and put a spoonful on top of the haddock before serving.

Health Benefits

White fish is a real winner in a low-fat diet. As well as being low in fat, fish is a protein-rich food, which helps to satisfy the appetite for longer than carbohydrate-based foods, making it an excellent start to the day.

Food Facts per Portion

Calories 226kcal • Total Fat 3.3g • saturated fat 0.5g

Soufflé Tuna Omelette

o

Whisking the egg whites increases their volume significantly. This means that fewer eggs are needed, as they go much further, which helps to keep the fat and calories down. Serve with slices of fresh crusty bread.

| **SERVES** 2 | **PREPARATION** 10 minutes | **COOKING** 5 minutes |

2 eggs, separated

1 tsp sunflower oil

40g/1½oz tinned tuna in water, drained and flaked

3 tbsp snipped fresh chives

salt and freshly ground black pepper

4 vine-ripened tomatoes, sliced

1   Whisk the egg whites in a large, grease-free bowl until they form stiff peaks. Beat the egg yolks in another large bowl. Season, then add the egg whites and carefully fold in using a metal spoon.

2   Gently heat the oil in a medium, heavy-based frying pan over a medium heat and swirl it around to cover the base. Spoon in the whisked, frothy egg mixture and gently flatten it using a spatula (without losing too much of the air) until it covers the base of the pan. Cook for 2 minutes.

3   Spread the tuna along the centre of the omelette and cook
for a further minute or so until the bottom of the omelette is
set and golden. Sprinkle with the chives then carefully fold
the omelette in half to encase the tuna.

4   Cut the omelette in half crossways, then transfer to two plates.
Add some sliced tomatoes and serve.

Health Benefits

Although eggs (specifically the yolk) do contain cholesterol, studies
suggest that they do not significantly affect cholesterol levels in
most individuals. Furthermore, eggs may improve the ratio of HDL
('good' cholesterol) to LDL ('bad' cholesterol). This has been
attributed to their monounsaturated fat content. An excellent source
of protein, eggs provide all the amino acids necessary for good
health and are also rich in immune-boosting nutrients such as zinc,
iron and selenium.

Food Facts per Portion

Calories 132kcal • Total Fat 7.6g • saturated fat 1.9g

Mozzarella & Tomato Stacks

This breakfast couldn't be easier to make but looks special enough to serve to weekend guests. Light mayonnaise is a valuable addition to the store cupboard, and, unlike many other lower-fat alternatives to high-fat foods, it is not full of additives to make up for the reduction in fat. It also makes a useful base for quick sauces, dips and marinades.

SERVES 4   **PREPARATION** 10 minutes

4 large vine-ripened tomatoes, each one cut into 3 thick slices and deseeded

150g/5½oz ball light mozzarella cheese, cut into 8 slices

1 tbsp light pesto

1 tbsp light mayonnaise

handful torn fresh basil, to scatter

salt and freshly ground black pepper

1 Put a slice of tomato on a plate and top with a slice of mozzarella, followed by a second slice of tomato and mozzarella, then a final slice of tomato. Repeat to prepare 4 servings.

2 Mix together the pesto, mayonnaise and 2 tsp water, and season. Spoon the pesto dressing over the stop of each tomato tower, scatter over a few basil leaves, then serve.

Health Benefits

Mozzarella is a naturally low-fat cheese containing around 18.5g/ $^3/_4$oz fat (12g/$^1/_2$ oz saturated fat) per 100g/3$^1/_2$ oz, but it is also possible to buy even lower-fat versions, called 'light'. As with other dairy products, mozzarella is rich in calcium. Best known for its beneficial effect on bone health, improving strength and density, calcium is also important for cell function and blood clotting.

Food Facts per Portion

Calories 152kcal • Total Fat 10.9g • saturated fat 5.5g

Griddled Tomatoes on Toast

The combination of soda bread and griddled tomatoes works particularly well and couldn't be easier to prepare, making it ideal if you are looking for something quick and warm to start the day. You could also add a sprinkling of shaved Parmesan cheese or a few fresh basil leaves. If cooking for more than one person, increase the quantity of ingredients accordingly.

SERVES 1   **PREPARATION** 5 minutes   **COOKING** 3 minutes

2 vine-ripened tomatoes, thickly sliced

½ tsp olive oil

2 tsp balsamic vinegar

1 thick slice soda bread

salt and freshly ground black pepper

1   Heat a griddle pan until hot. Brush one side of the tomato slices with half of the olive oil and cook for 1 minute, then brush the uncooked sides, turn the tomatoes over and cook for another minute. Pour the balsamic vinegar over the tomatoes and heat briefly.

2   Meanwhile, lightly toast the bread, then put on a plate. Arrange the sliced tomatoes on top and pour over any juices left in the pan. Season and serve.

Health Benefits

Lycopene, a carotenoid responsible for the red colour of tomatoes, is a potent antioxidant that has been linked to a reduced risk of diseases such as cardiovascular disease, cancer, diabetes and osteoporosis, as well as male infertility. Lycopene is more potent when the tomatoes are cooked.

Food Facts per Portion

Calories 114kcal • Total Fat 3.1g • saturated fat 0.7g

Variations

Experiment with different types of bread, including sourdough, mixed grain, bagel or ciabatta.

Avocado & Black Olive Toast

Avocados are a perhaps surprising substitute for high-fat butter, but thanks to their rich flavour and creamy texture, they make a delicious alternative. Avocados have had some bad press due to their fat content, but bear in mind that it is the beneficial monounsaturated type of fat, and don't forget about their wealth of other beneficial nutrients (see opposite).

SERVES 1   **PREPARATION** 7 minutes   **COOKING** 2 minutes

1 thick slice wholegrain bread

½ small avocado, pitted

½ tsp light mayonnaise

½ tsp lemon juice

1 vine-ripened tomato, deseeded and diced

3 pitted black olives, sliced

few torn fresh basil leaves, to scatter

salt and freshly ground black pepper

1   Toast the bread on both sides.

2   Meanwhile, scoop the avocado flesh out of its skin into a bowl, add the mayonnaise and lemon juice and mash together. Stir in the diced tomato and season to taste.

3   Spoon the mixture over the toast, then top with the black olives. Scatter over the basil before serving.

Health Benefits

Avocados are not only a rich source of monounsaturated fatty acids (including oleic acid, which has recently been shown to reduce the risk of breast cancer) but also a good source of vitamins E, C and B6, folic acid, potassium and dietary fibre. The antioxidant lutein, which is found to benefit eye health, is also present in avocados in significant amounts.

Food Facts per Portion

Calories 171kcal • Total Fat 10.4g • saturated fat 2.3g

Variation

Try reduced-fat humous (flavoured with lemon, spices or chilli) in place of the avocado, mayonnaise and lemon mixture. Spread it on the toast, then scatter with the tomatoes and olives. Season and top with the basil.

Eggs en Cocotte

V O 🍳

Eggs fortified with omega-3 are now readily available in shops. Vegetarians, in particular, may find this a useful way of boosting their intake of this essential fatty acid, which can be obtained only through diet. Make sure you squeeze out as much water from the spinach as possible after steaming to avoid a watery residue at the bottom of each ramekin.

SERVES 4	PREPARATION 10 minutes	COOKING 17 minutes

rapeseed oil, for greasing

400g/14oz/4½ cups spinach, tough stalks removed, rinsed well

2 tsp Dijon mustard

4 eggs

2 tbsp quark

1 tbsp snipped fresh chives (optional)

salt and freshly ground black pepper

1 Preheat the oven to 180°C/350°F/Gas 4. Lightly grease four ramekin dishes, about 7.5cm/3in in diameter and 4cm/1½in deep, with the oil.

2 Steam the spinach for about 2 minutes until wilted and tender. Squeeze out any water and chop roughly. Stir the mustard into the spinach and divide it between the ramekins.

3 Break an egg into each dish, then top with half a tablespoon of quark; season to taste.

4 Put the ramekins in a roasting tin. Pour boiling water into the tin until it comes halfway up the sides of the ramekins. Bake in the preheated oven for 15 minutes, then remove the tin from the oven. Take care when removing the ramekins from the tin. Sprinkle with the chives, if using, and serve.

Health Benefits

Spinach is a superb source of cancer-fighting antioxidants and contains four times more beta carotene than broccoli. Along with vitamin C, beta carotene helps fight damaging free radicals in the body and the chronic diseases associated with the aging process. Spinach is also an excellent source of folic acid, required by the body to help reduce the effects of a potentially harmful chemical called homocysteine, which can lead to a heart attack or stroke if levels become too high.

Food Facts per Portion

Calories 110kcal • Total Fat 6.5g • saturated fat 1.7g

Boiled Egg with Asparagus

Packed with brain-boosting protein as well as energy-giving carbohydrate, a boiled egg served with crusty wholemeal bread and vitamin-rich asparagus makes an ideal start to the day. If asparagus is out of season, try steamed green beans instead.

SERVES 1   **PREPARATION** 8 minutes   **COOKING** 4 minutes

1 egg

6 asparagus spears, trimmed

salt and freshly ground black pepper

1 slice crusty wholemeal bread, to serve

1 Put the egg in a small saucepan of water and bring to the boil. Boil for about 4 minutes, or to your liking.

2 Meanwhile, steam the asparagus for about 3 minutes until tender.

3 Put the egg in an eggcup, cut off its top and season. Serve with the asparagus spears, for dipping into the yolk, and the bread.

Health Benefits

A known diuretic, asparagus is rich in vitamins and minerals, particularly potassium, iron and the B vitamin, folic acid, which is essential for a healthy heart and for the synthesis of DNA.

Food Facts per Portion

Calories 173kcal • Total Fat 7g • saturated fat 1.7g

Light Meals

There are occasions when we don't have the time or the inclination to spend a long time in the kitchen preparing a meal, and this can be when it's all too easy to grab that fat-loaded slice of quiche, sausage roll, portion of chips, pizza or hunk of cheese.

The recipes in this chapter aim to steer you away from this path and cover a diverse selection of meals for those occasions when you want something quick and easy to prepare that is fresh, light and, it goes without saying, low in fat. Suitable for both lunch and a light supper, there are recipes based on meat, poultry, fish and seafood, plus vegetarian dishes.

Choose from a zingy Thai-style Beef Salad, Tandoori Chicken or Cajun Salmon Roll. And who said you had to give up fast food? You'll find healthier, low-fat versions of popular fast-food dishes, such as a Provençal Pizza, Mexican-style Turkey Burgers and Chilli Beef Fajitas.

Soup is an obvious choice when it comes to perfect low-fat cooking, and this chapter contains some delicious options, such as Pea & Bacon Soup, Moroccan Chicken, Spinach & Chickpea Soup and the classic Thai Tom Yam Gai. Salads also come into their own here, as long as you don't go over the top with the dressings – and they include Crab Salad with Herb Mayo, Japanese-style Smoked Tofu Salad and Warm Chicken Salad with Avocado Dressing.

Char-grilled Asparagus with Prosciutto

It's really worth investing in a ridged griddle pan, as this method of cooking not only requires the minimum amount of oil but also adds a wonderful 'smoky' flavour to foods. Serve with crusty sourdough bread.

SERVES 4   **PREPARATION** 10 minutes   **COOKING** 10 minutes

24 asparagus spears, trimmed

2 tsp olive oil

4 tsp balsamic vinegar

8 slices prosciutto, trimmed of fat

Tomato salad:

8 vine-ripened tomatoes, thinly sliced

juice of 1/2 small lemon

1/2 tsp dried oregano

salt and freshly ground black pepper

1 Put the tomatoes in a serving bowl and squeeze over the lemon juice. Scatter with the oregano and season to taste. Set aside.

2 Heat a large griddle pan until hot. Lightly brush the asparagus with the oil, then put half of the spears in the pan. Cook for 4 minutes, turning once or twice, then remove to a warm plate with a fish slice. Cook the second batch of asparagus in the same way.

3 While the second batch is cooking, brush the cooked asparagus with half of the balsamic vinegar, then wrap a slice of prosciutto around 3 spears; repeat to give 4 bundles. Repeat with the second batch of asparagus and remaining balsamic vinegar and prosciutto.

4 Return half of the asparagus bundles to the pan and cook over a medium-high heat, turning once, for about 1 minute until lightly browned. Remove from the griddle pan and keep warm. Repeat with the remaining asparagus bundles. Serve 2 asparagus bundles per person with the tomato salad.

Storage

The asparagus can be stored in an airtight container in the refrigerator for up to 2 days, then served cold (but not chilled: remove from the refrigerator 1 hour before serving).

Health Benefits

Asparagus is a good source of folate – the B vitamin that keeps the nerves and arteries in good shape. It also contains glutathione – an important antioxidant that helps the liver to clear out toxins.

Food Facts per Portion

Calories 99kcal · Total Fat 4.4g · saturated fat 0.9g

Pea & Bacon Soup

Peas, bacon and mint are a classic combination, and this soup uses them to make a light yet sustaining lunch. Frozen peas are used instead of fresh, since they are available all year round and are just as good, if not better, nutritionally. Furthermore, they allow you to rustle up this soup in a matter of minutes.

SERVES 4   **PREPARATION** 10 minutes   **COOKING** 25–30 minutes

1 tbsp olive oil

1 large onion, diced

450g/1lb/2 large potatoes, peeled and cut into chunks

2 carrots, scrubbed and sliced

2 celery sticks, sliced

1.2 litres/2 pints/5 cups vegetable stock

2 bay leaves

1 bouquet garni

2 lean back/Canadian bacon rashers, trimmed of fat

500g/1lb 2oz/4$\frac{1}{3}$ cups frozen peas

2 tbsp 1% fat milk

3 tbsp chopped fresh mint , to scatter

salt and freshly ground black pepper

1   Heat the oil in a large saucepan and sauté the onion, stirring occasionally, for 5 minutes until softened. Add the potatoes, carrots and celery and cook, stirring, for another minute.

2   Add the stock, bay leaves and bouquet garni and bring to
the boil, then reduce the heat and simmer, half-covered,
for 10 minutes or until the potatoes are tender.

3   Preheat the grill, then cook the bacon for 5–7 minutes until
crisp, turning halfway.

4   While the bacon is grilling, add the peas to the soup. Return to
the boil, then reduce the heat and simmer for 2–3 minutes
until all of the vegetables are cooked.

5   Remove the bay leaves and bouquet garni, then, using a stick
blender, blender or food processor, purée the soup until smooth.
Return the soup to the heat and stir in the crème fraîche, then
season to taste; if the soup is too thick add a little extra stock.

6   Using scissors, snip the grilled bacon into small pieces, then
scatter over the soup with the mint before serving.

Storage
Can be stored in an airtight container in the refrigerator for up to
3 days, then reheated.

Health Benefits
A good source of low-fat protein and fibre, peas are also rich in
vitamin C, iron, thiamine, folate and potassium.

Food Facts per Portion
Calories 234kcal • Total Fat 4.5g • saturated fat 0.8g

Glazed Pork in Lettuce Wraps

Marinades are an excellent way of adding plenty of flavour to fish, meat and vegetables without the need for much extra oil.

SERVES 4

PREPARATION 15 minutes, plus marinating   **COOKING** 3 minutes

350g/12oz lean pork loin fillets, trimmed of any fat and thinly sliced

4 Romaine lettuce leaves

2 large spring onions/scallions, shredded

1 small cucumber, deseeded and sliced into strips

2 tsp light mayonnaise

2 tsp sweet chilli sauce

small handful fresh coriander/cilantro, chopped

salt and freshly ground black pepper

For the marinade:

1 tsp Sichuan peppercorns

3 tbsp soy sauce

4 tbsp fresh orange juice

$\frac{1}{2}$ tsp sesame oil

2.5cm/1in piece fresh root ginger, peeled and grated

1   To make the marinade, put the peppercorns in a dry frying pan and heat gently until they start to smell toasted, then remove from the heat. Grind in a grinder or using a pestle and mortar

until they form a coarse powder, then mix with the soy sauce, orange juice and sesame oil in a large shallow dish. Squeeze the juice from the grated ginger into the dish and discard the pulp. Add the pork to the dish and leave to marinate for about 1 hour.

2 Heat a large non-stick frying pan and add the pork, reserving the marinade. Cook for about 2 minutes, turning the pork, then add the marinade and cook for another minute until it begins to thicken and the pork becomes golden and glossy.

3 Open out the lettuce leaves and divide the pork and any remaining marinade in the pan between them. Top with the spring onions/scallions and cucumber.

4 Mix together the mayonnaise and sweet chilli sauce and put a teaspoonful of the mixture on top of the pork mixture. Season to taste and scatter with the coriander/cilantro. Serve the wraps as they are or roll up each lettuce leaf to enclose the filling.

Storage
The pork can be marinated and cooked in advance, then stored in an airtight container in the refrigerator for up to 2 days.

Health Benefits
Salad leaves are primarily eaten raw, which means they retain their nutrients, especially vitamin C, beta carotene and folic acid.

Food Facts per Portion
Calories 176kcal • Total Fat 4.7g • saturated fat 1.5g

Pasta with Lamb & Rocket

Red meat provides many health benefits, but due to its fat content it should be eaten in moderation – well, at least not included in the diet every day. This southern Italian-style dish can also be made with beef or chicken.

SERVES 4   **PREPARATION** 15 minutes   **COOKING** 15 minutes

2 lean boneless lamb steaks, about 150g/5½oz each

8 shallots, thinly sliced

3 garlic cloves, roughly chopped

2 tsp olive oil

350g/12oz tagliatelle

1 tbsp lemon juice

4 large handfuls wild rocket

salt and freshly ground black pepper

1   Preheat the grill to high. Put the lamb, shallots and garlic in a dish and pour over the oil, then turn to coat them in the oil.

2   Grill the lamb under the preheated grill for 3–4 minutes, then turn the meat over, baste with any juices in the bottom of the pan and grill for another 3–4 minutes. Remove from the grill, cover and leave to rest.

3   While the lamb is grilling and resting, cook the pasta in plenty of boiling salted water following the packet instructions. Drain the pasta, reserving 4 tablespoons of the water, and return to the pan.

4   Heat a non-stick frying pan and add the shallots and garlic with any oil remaining in the dish. Fry for 5 minutes, stirring frequently, until softened and slightly golden. Add a splash of water if the pan appears dry.

5   Thinly slice the lamb and add to the pasta with the shallots, garlic, lemon juice, reserved cooking water and any juices in the grill pan. Season and toss until combined.

6   Divide the pasta between four bowls and scatter with the rocket before serving.

Health Benefits

Grinding black pepper over your meal is reputed to help the body absorb nutrients from food more efficiently. Keep an eye on your salt intake, though: according to research, reducing intake by 2.5g/$\frac{1}{16}$ oz a day would reduce the risk of a heart attack or stroke by a quarter.

Food Facts per Portion

Calories 473kcal • Total Fat 10g • saturated fat 3.1g

Thai-style Beef Salad

Fresh fragrant herbs and a zingy, fat-free dressing add bundles of flavour to this char-grilled beef salad. It is also a great way of using beef you have left over from a roast. Serve with warm flatbreads or toss with some cooked rice or egg noodles.

SERVES 4   **PREPARATION** 15 minutes   **COOKING** 4 minutes

400g/14oz lean rump or sirloin steak

1 tsp sunflower oil, for greasing

3 Little Gem lettuces, trimmed and leaves separated

4 shallots, finely sliced

2 yellow bell peppers, deseeded and sliced

10 cherry tomatoes, halved

1 long red chilli, deseeded and finely sliced

handful fresh coriander/cilantro, to scatter

handful torn fresh basil, to scatter

freshly ground black pepper

Dressing:

juice of 2 limes

1 tsp sugar

1 small garlic clove, crushed

3 tbsp fish sauce

4 tbsp light soy sauce

1 Heat a griddle pan until hot. Toss the steak in the oil, then season with black pepper. Char-grill the steak for 3–4 minutes, turning once, or until cooked to your liking. Remove from the pan and leave to rest for 10 minutes, then slice thinly across the grain.

2 Arrange the lettuce leaves in four shallow dishes and top with the beef. Scatter the shallots, yellow bell peppers, tomatoes and chilli over the top.

3 To make the dressing, mix the lime juice with the sugar and stir until the sugar has dissolved. Stir in the garlic, fish sauce and soy sauce. Pour the dressing over the salad. Season, and scatter the coriander and basil over the salad.

Health Benefits
Lean steak is an excellent source of protein, which is needed for the continuous repair and maintenance of the body, as well as being one of the best suppliers of iron – a mineral crucial for transporting oxygen to the cells.

Food Facts per Portion
Calories 181kcal • Total Fat 5.6g • saturated fat 2.1g

Chilli Beef Fajitas

Here, strips of beef are cooked in a blend of spices with onions and peppers, then served on top of a warm tortilla to give a flavoursome Mexican-style lunch. Serve with a green salad.

SERVES 4   **PREPARATION** 15 minutes   **COOKING** 10 minutes

2 tsp olive oil

2 red onions, sliced

1 red bell pepper, deseeded and sliced

½ tsp crushed dried chillies

1 tsp paprika

1 tsp cumin seeds

300g/10½oz lean beef fillet, cut into thin strips

4 soft wholemeal tortillas

6 crisp lettuce leaves, shredded

3 tomatoes, diced

juice of 1 lime

2 tbsp 0% fat Greek yogurt

2 tbsp chopped fresh coriander/cilantro, to scatter

salt and freshly ground black pepper

1   Heat the oil in a large, non-stick frying pan and fry the onions
    for 5 minutes. Add the red bell pepper and cook for another
    3 minutes, adding a splash of water if the pan appears dry.
    Add the spices, then the beef, and season. Cook, stirring
    frequently, for another 2 minutes.

2   Meanwhile, warm the tortillas, 2 at a time, in a separate dry
    frying pan for 2 minutes, turning occasionally.

3   To serve, put a tortilla on each plate. Put the lettuce on top, then
    the beef mixture, then the tomatoes. Squeeze the lime juice over
    and add a spoonful of the yogurt. Scatter with the coriander/
    cilantro before serving.

Health Benefits

Onions have long been recognized for their numerous health
benefits. They contain allicin, which has been found to stimulate
the body's fight against free radicals as well as raising levels of
HDL (beneficial cholesterol) and reducing LDL (harmful cholesterol), so protecting the heart.

Food Facts per Portion

Calories 232kcal • Total Fat 6.9g • saturated fat 2.4g

Open Club Sandwich

O 🌢 🍃

Crisp prosciutto, succulent chicken breast and crisp lettuce make a substantial topping for this open sandwich. For a more filling meal, serve with a mixed bean and fresh herb salad.

SERVES 2   **PREPARATION** 10 minutes   **COOKING** 2 minutes

2 slices prosciutto, trimmed of fat

2 thick slices wholemeal bread

1 tsp light mayonnaise

2 large, crisp lettuce leaves

2 slices skinless cooked chicken breast, about 100g/3^{1}/$_{2}$oz total weight

squeeze of fresh lemon juice

2 vine-ripened tomatoes, sliced

salt and freshly ground black pepper

1   Preheat the grill to high. Grill the prosciutto for about 2 minutes, turning once, until crisp. Meanwhile, toast the bread on one side.

2   Put a slice of bread, toasted-side down, on each plate. Spread the non-toasted side with the mayonnaise, then season.

3   Cover each slice with a lettuce leaf and a slice of chicken, then squeeze over a little lemon juice. Place the tomatoes and prosciutto on top, then serve.

Health Benefits

Fibre, which is found in wholemeal bread and other wholegrain foods, can help you to reduce your calorie intake without leaving you hungry. This is because such foods are naturally filling, helping to curb the appetite.

Food Facts per Portion

Calories 170kcal • Total Fat 3.4g • saturated fat 0.8g

Variations

For a vegetarian alternative, replace the prosciutto and chicken with half an avocado, mashed with the lemon juice, then top with a grilled rasher of vegetarian bacon. Another option is to mash a small tin of drained cannellini beans with a crushed garlic clove, a small handful of chopped parsley and the lemon juice. Top with the tomatoes before serving.

Tom Yam Gai

Thai soups are packed with flavour and are remarkably low in fat. They vary in substance from a light broth to this version, which includes noodles, chicken and fresh vegetables to make a filling, nutritious soup.

SERVES 4   **PREPARATION** 15 minutes   **COOKING** 12 minutes

875ml/30fl oz/3½ cups vegetable stock

2 lemongrass sticks, peeled and crushed using the back of a knife

1 large red chilli, finely chopped

4 kaffir lime leaves

2 garlic cloves, finely sliced

4 spring onions/scallions, finely sliced

juice of 1 lime

1 tbsp fish sauce

1 carrot, peeled and cut into fine strips

1 red bell pepper, deseeded and finely sliced

400g/14oz ready-cooked thin rice noodles

400g/14oz cooked skinless chicken breasts, cut into thick slices

handful fresh coriander/cilantro, chopped, to scatter

salt and freshly ground black pepper

1   Put the stock in a saucepan with the lemongrass, half of the chilli, the kaffir lime leaves, garlic and half of the spring onions/ scallions. Bring to the boil, then reduce the heat and simmer, half-covered, for 10 minutes.

2   Strain the stock and discard the solids, then season to taste. Stir in the lime juice and fish sauce.

3   Divide the remaining chilli and spring onions/scallions, the carrot, red bell pepper, rice noodles and chicken between four bowls. Pour the stock into the bowls and scatter with the coriander/cilantro before serving.

Storage

The stock can be made up to 2 days in advance. Reheat and follow step 3.

Health Benefits

Chicken contains very little fat in comparison to other types of meat, but do remember to remove the skin and prepare it in a way to keep fat levels to a minimum, such as in this soup. This high-quality protein food is rich in vitamins E and B, particularly niacin and thiamine, which are essential for energy production.

Food Facts per Portion

Calories 525kcal • Total Fat 2.7g • saturated fat 0.6g

Chicken Soup

Nourishing and filling, this simple soup is a complete meal in itself. The milk adds a slight creaminess, but can be left out if preferred. Serve the soup with crusty bread or rolls.

SERVES 4   **PREPARATION** 10 minutes   **COOKING** 30–35 minutes

1 tbsp olive oil

1 large onion, finely chopped

1 celery stick, sliced

1 large carrot, peeled and chopped

350g/12oz skinless boneless chicken breast, cubed

1.25 litres/44fl oz/5 cups chicken stock

2 large potatoes, peeled and cubed

2 bay leaves

1 tsp dried thyme

4 tbsp skimmed milk

salt and freshly ground black pepper

1   Heat the oil in a large saucepan and sauté the onion, celery and carrot for 5 minutes, half-covered, until softened.

2   Add the chicken and sauté for another 3–4 minutes until sealed and light golden on all sides.

3 Pour in the stock, add the potatoes, bay leaves and thyme
and bring to the boil, then reduce the heat and simmer,
half-covered, for 20–25 minutes until the chicken is cooked
and potatoes are tender. Stir in the milk and season to taste
before serving.

Storage

Can be stored in an airtight container in the refrigerator for up to
2 days, then reheated.

Health Benefits

Like asparagus, celery was once grown solely for medicinal reasons.
Low in calories, yet a good source of vitamin C, celery is recognized
for its diuretic and soporific qualities.

Food Facts per Portion

Calories 221kcal • Total Fat 4.7g • saturated fat 0.9g

Variation

Instead of the potatoes, you could add tinned beans, such as
cannellini, or cooked pearl barley.

Moroccan Chicken, Spinach & Chickpea Soup

This hearty soup needs little in the way of an accompaniment and tastes just as good – if not better – if made the day before serving. Turn it into a delicious vegetarian soup by omitting the chicken and doubling the quantity of chickpeas/garbanzo beans.

SERVES 4   **PREPARATION** 10 minutes   **COOKING** 35 minutes

2 tsp olive oil

1 large red onion, sliced

250g/9oz skinless boneless chicken breasts, cubed

2 garlic cloves, chopped

2 tsp cumin seeds

1 tbsp ras el hanout

1.5 litres/52fl oz/6 cups vegetable stock

200g/7oz tinned chickpeas/garbanzo beans in water, drained and rinsed

400g/14oz spinach, tough stalks removed, rinsed well and shredded

handful fresh coriander/cilantro

1 tsp lime juice

salt and freshly ground black pepper

1   Heat the oil in a large saucepan and sauté the onion,
    half-covered, for 5 minutes until softened. Add the chicken and
    sauté for another 3–4 minutes until sealed and light golden on
    all sides.

2   Add the garlic and spices and cook for another minute, then
    pour in the stock. Bring to the boil, then reduce the heat and
    simmer, half-covered, for 10 minutes.

3   Add the chickpeas/garbanzo beans, spinach and coriander/
    cilantro and cook for another 10 minutes. Stir in the lime juice
    and season to taste before serving.

Storage

Can be stored in an airtight container in the refrigerator for up to
2 days, then reheated.

Health Benefits

The super nutrient, lutein, is found in significant amounts in spinach.
This yellow pigment has been found to be effective in fighting age-
related blindness. Research has found that 10mg lutein a day
appears to protect the skin against premature ageing and
improving hydration, and just 100g/3½oz spinach provides 13mg.

Food Facts per Portion

Calories 195kcal • Total Fat 5.4g • saturated fat 0.8g

Tandoori Chicken

A blend of spices, yogurt and tomatoes makes an excellent low-fat marinade and keeps the chicken succulent without the need for copious amounts of oil. The chicken is served simply here with a warmed chapatti and a spoonful of raita, though a simple crisp green salad would also work well.

SERVES 4

PREPARATION 15 minutes, plus marinating   **COOKING** 20 minutes

2 tbsp tandoori spice blend

1/2 tsp chilli powder

100ml/31/2fl oz/scant 1/2 cup low-fat natural bio yogurt

1 garlic clove, crushed

1 tbsp lime juice

2 tomatoes, deseeded

1 tsp sunflower oil

4 skinless boneless chicken breasts, about 150g/51/2oz each,
    with 3 diagonal slashes cut in each

4 wholemeal chapatti, warmed, to serve

Raita:

100ml/31/2fl oz/scant 1/2 cup low-fat natural bio yogurt

juice and finely grated zest of 1 lime

4cm/11/2in piece cucumber, finely diced

salt and freshly ground black pepper

1 Put the tandoori spice blend, chilli powder, yogurt, garlic, lime juice, tomatoes and oil in a blender and process until puréed. Put the chicken in a shallow dish, cover with the tandoori marinade and turn until coated. Cover and leave to marinate in the refrigerator for at least 1 hour or overnight if time allows.

2 Preheat the oven to 200°C/400°F/Gas 6. Arrange the chicken in a non-stick roasting tin and spoon over the marinade. Roast for 10 minutes, then turn over and cover the top with any remaining marinade and roast for a further 10 minutes until cooked through and there is no trace of pink in the centre.

3 While the chicken is cooking, mix together the ingredients for the raita and season to taste. Serve the chicken with the warm chapatti and a spoonful of raita.

Storage

The cooked chicken can be stored in an airtight container in the refrigerator for up to 1 day, then served cold.

Health Benefits

Yogurt helps to ensure the digestive system remains healthy, strengthening and supporting the immune system. It is also rich in potassium, calcium and B vitamins.

Food Facts per Portion

Calories 379kcal • Total Fat 5.5g • saturated fat 1.4g

Warm Chicken & Lentil Salad

Tinned lentils make a great store-cupboard standby and a convenient base for a salad, soup or stew. The vegetables in this salad are cooked lightly to retain their crisp, crunchy texture and valuable nutrients.

SERVES 4   **PREPARATION** 15 minutes   **COOKING** 12 minutes

1 tbsp olive oil

400g/14oz skinless boneless chicken breasts, cut into strips

1 large red bell pepper, deseeded and diced

5 spring onions/scallions, sliced

2 celery sticks, sliced

1 red chilli, chopped

800g/28oz tinned green lentils in water, drained and rinsed

1 tbsp Dijon mustard

2 tbsp lemon juice

finely grated zest of 1 small lemon

3 tbsp 0% fat Greek yogurt

handful torn fresh basil, to scatter

salt and freshly ground black pepper

1   Heat the oil in a non-stick sauté pan and fry the chicken over
    a medium heat for about 6–8 minutes, turning regularly, until
    slightly golden and cooked through. Remove from the pan
    and drain on kitchen paper.

2   Add the red bell pepper, spring onions/scallions and celery to
    the pan and sauté over a medium-low heat for 2 minutes, then
    stir in the chilli, lentils, mustard, lemon juice and zest, yogurt
    and 2 tablespoons water. Return the chicken to the pan and
    stir until everything is combined, then warm through for about
    1–2 minutes.

3   Season the salad to taste, then divide between four plates
    and scatter over the basil before serving.

Health Benefits

Green lentils provide an impressive range of nutritional benefits.
Extremely low in fat and richer in protein than most pulses, lentils
have been found to reduce LDL (harmful cholesterol) in the body,
consequently protecting the heart. Lentils are also rich in fibre,
helping the efficiency of the bowels and colon.

Food Facts per Portion

Calories 298kcal • Total Fat 5.8g • saturated fat 1.1g

Chicken & Chickpea Salad

⏺ ▶ ☺

This substantial salad combines low-fat, protein-rich chicken
and fibre-rich chickpeas/garbanzo beans with a creamy dressing.

SERVES 4   **PREPARATION** 10 minutes   **COOKING** 6–8 minutes

450g/1lb skinless boneless chicken breasts, sliced into strips

1 tbsp olive oil

150g/5^{1}/$_{2}$oz spinach, rocket and watercress salad

1 small avocado, pitted, peeled and cubed

4 vine-ripened tomatoes, thinly sliced

400g/14oz tinned chickpeas/garbanzo beans in water,
    drained and rinsed

Dressing:

1 tbsp light mayonnaise

1 tbsp light pesto

juice of ½ lemon

salt and freshly ground black pepper

1   Heat a griddle pan until hot. Brush the chicken with the oil,
    then char-grill for 6–8 minutes, turning once, until cooked
    through and golden. Leave to cool slightly.

2   While the chicken is cooking, make the dressing. Mix together
    the mayonnaise, pesto and lemon juice. Add 1 tablespoon warm
    water and stir until combined. Season to taste.

3 Put the salad leaves, avocado, tomatoes, chickpeas/garbanzo beans and chicken in a salad bowl and spoon over the dressing.

Health Benefits

Soluble fibre found in pulses, such as chickpeas/garbanzo beans, becomes a sticky, glue-like substance in the gut. When this happens, it helps us to feel full for longer as well as having a beneficial effect on cholesterol and blood-sugar levels.

Food Facts per Portion

Calories 352kcal • Total Fat 13.1g • saturated fat 2.2g

Variation

Any type of tinned bean or lentil would work well in this recipe – try cannellini, flageolet or butter beans for starters.

Warm Chicken Salad with Avocado Dressing

Avocados get a bad press due to their reputedly high fat content, yet this is unfairly so since it is beneficial monounsaturated fat, shown to reduce levels of harmful cholesterol in the body. Avocados also provide useful amounts of vitamin E.

SERVES 4   **PREPARATION** 15 minutes   **COOKING** 12–20 minutes

4 skinless boneless chicken breasts, about 150g/5½oz each

1 tbsp olive oil

1 yellow bell pepper, deseeded and sliced

150g/5½oz mixed salad leaves

16 cherry tomatoes, halved

handful mixed sprouted seeds and beans

3 spring onions/scallions, thinly sliced on the diagonal

handful torn fresh basil

salt and freshly ground black pepper

Dressing:

1 small avocado, peeled, pitted and chopped

juice and finely grated zest of 1 lime

5 tbsp virtually fat-free fromage frais

½ tsp crushed dried chillies (optional)

1   Put each chicken breast between 2 sheets of cling film and flatten with the end of a rolling pin. Lightly brush the chicken with the oil and season.

2   Heat a griddle pan and char-grill the chicken in 2 batches for about 2–4 minutes on each side, depending on the thickness of the fillets, until cooked through.

3   Remove the chicken from the pan, then add the bell pepper and char-grill for about 3 minutes, turning once, until just blackened.

4   Meanwhile, to make the dressing, put the avocado, lime zest and juice, fromage frais and crushed dried chillies, if using, in a blender and blend. Season well.

5   Arrange the salad leaves on four plates, then add the pepper, tomatoes, sprouted seeds and beans and spring onions/scallions. Slice the chicken and add to the salad. Spoon the dressing over, then scatter with the basil before serving.

Health Benefits

Sprouted seeds and beans are bursting with nutrients. Once they have germinated, their nutritional value rises significantly; they provide almost 30 per cent more B vitamins and 60 per cent more vitamin C than seeds or beans that have not yet sprouted.

Food Facts per Portion

Calories 319kcal • Total Fat 9g • saturated fat 2.1g

Thai Chicken, Cucumber & Mango Salad

Thai food is an evocative combination of sweet, sour, hot and salty flavours – all without the need for large amounts of oil. In fact, the dressing for this salad is completely fat-free. The peanuts are optional but do add flavour and crunch to this simple salad. Serve with egg noodles.

SERVES 4   **PREPARATION** 15 minutes   **COOKING** 6–8 minutes

450g/1lb skinless chicken breasts, cut into 1cm/½in strips

300g/10½oz/scant 1 cup fresh mango chunks, drained, reserving 1 tbsp juice

2 handfuls watercress

1 small cucumber, deseeded and sliced into half-moons

1 tbsp roasted peanuts (optional)

handful fresh coriander/cilantro, to scatter

Dressing:

2 tbsp fish sauce

4 tbsp lime juice

1 small garlic clove, crushed

½ tsp crushed dried chillies

1   Preheat the grill to medium-high. Grill the chicken strips for
    6–8 minutes, turning once, until cooked through.

2   Put the reserved mango juice and all the dressing ingredients
    in a bowl and mix together.

3   Arrange the mango, watercress, cucumber and chicken on a
    serving plate. Spoon the dressing over the salad. Scatter with
    the peanuts, if using, and the coriander/cilantro leaves.

Health Benefits

Mangoes contain digestive enzymes that help to break down
proteins and aid digestion. Rich in vitamin C and beta carotene,
this golden-fleshed fruit is also a good source of B vitamins,
potassium and magnesium.

Food Facts per Portion

Calories 242kcal • Total Fat 4.8g • saturated fat 1.2g

Cool Dogs

❶ ❷ ❸

Children will love this healthier version of a hot dog using turkey strips and a soft wholemeal tortilla, instead of the usual processed sausage and white bun. You could also use cooked turkey left over from a roast. Serve with a fruit smoothie for a delicious light lunch – it would also make a great addition to a lunchbox.

SERVES 4   **PREPARATION** 10 minutes   **COOKING** 6–8 minutes

450g/1lb skinless turkey breast, cut into 4cm/1½in strips

2 tsp olive oil

1 tbsp sweet chilli sauce

1 tbsp light mayonnaise

4 small wholemeal tortillas

4 vine-ripened tomatoes, deseeded and diced

1 spring onion/scallion, finely sliced (optional)

salt and freshly ground black pepper

1   Preheat the grill to high. Brush the turkey strips with the oil, then grill for 6–8 minutes, turning once, until cooked through.

2   Meanwhile, mix together the sweet chilli sauce and mayonnaise.

3   Warm the tortillas under the grill (which will still be warm from cooking the turkey), then slice each one in half. Spread each half with a little of the mayonnaise mixture.

4 Put a few strips of turkey crossways on the top of each half of tortilla. Spoon over the tomatoes and top with the spring onion/scallion, if using, then roll up each tortilla half to encase the turkey filling. Serve warm or cold.

Health Benefits

Turkey is a good source of protein, B vitamins, folic acid and zinc. These nutrients have been found to keep blood cholesterol down, protect against cancer and heart disease, boost the immune system, regulate blood pressure and assist in healing processes.

Food Facts per Portion

Calories 279kcal • Total Fat 5g • saturated fat 1.2g

Mexican-style Turkey Burgers

Children will love these lightly spiced burgers, which really are very straightforward to make.

SERVES 4   **PREPARATION** 15 minutes   **COOKING** 12–16 minutes

400g/14oz lean turkey mince

1 onion, grated

1 tbsp fajita spice mix

1 small egg, lightly beaten

flour, for dusting

1 tsp sunflower oil

salt and freshly ground black pepper

To serve:

4 wholemeal rolls, split and lightly toasted

2 tomatoes, sliced

4 crisp lettuce leaves

2 tbsp sweet chilli sauce

1   Put the turkey in a large mixing bowl with the onion and fajita spice mix. Season to taste and stir in the egg. Dust a plate with flour. Using wet hands, divide the mince mixture into 4 portions and form each portion into a round, flat burger, then dust with a little flour.

2 Heat the grill to medium-high. Put the burgers in the grill pan and brush the top with half of the oil. Grill for 6–8 minutes, then turn and brush with the remaining oil and cook for another 6–8 minutes or until cooked through.

3 Put a lettuce leaf, a few slices of tomato and a spoonful of sweet chilli sauce on one half of each roll, then top with a burger and the second half of roll, and serve.

Storage

The uncooked burgers can be stored in an airtight container in the refrigerator for up to 1 day or in the freezer for up to 1 month. To prevent the burgers sticking together, put a piece of greaseproof/waxed paper between them.

Health Benefits

An excellent source of low-fat protein, turkey also provides immune-boosting zinc as well as selenium – an important mineral that zaps free radicals and protects against inhaled pollutants.

Food Facts per Portion

Calories 335kcal • Total Fat 10.8g • saturated fat 2.9g

Variation

The burger mixture would also work well made into little meatballs and cooked in a tomato sauce. Just dust them in flour and brown in some oil in a pan before adding to a tomato sauce, then simmer for 20 minutes.

Cajun Salmon Roll

The Cajun spices add an interesting twist to a simple fillet of salmon and help to cut through the oiliness of the fish. Once cooked, use the salmon as a filling for a crusty brown roll. Serve with sticks of carrot, celery and red bell pepper.

SERVES 1   **PREPARATION** 5 minutes   **COOKING** 6–10 minutes

squeeze of fresh lemon juice

100g/3$\frac{1}{2}$oz skinless salmon fillet, sliced into strips

$\frac{1}{4}$–$\frac{1}{2}$ tsp Cajun spice blend or fajita spice mix

crusty brown roll

1 tsp light mayonnaise

1 crisp lettuce leaf, sliced into strips

5 slices cucumber

salt and freshly ground black pepper

1   Preheat the grill to high. Squeeze the lemon juice over the salmon in a shallow dish, then sprinkle the spice blend over the top of the fillet.

2   Cook the salmon, spice-side up first, under the preheated grill for 3–5 minutes on each side, turning once, until cooked through.

3   Cut the roll in half and spread one side with the mayonnaise. Add the lettuce and cucumber, then place the salmon on top. Season. Top with the other half of the roll, then serve.

Health Benefits

Salmon provides beneficial amounts of omega-3 fatty acids, which help to reduce inflammation associated with arthritis, and also play a role in regulating blood pressure, potentially helping to reduce the risk of heart disease.

Food Facts per Portion

Calories 316kcal • Total Fat 14.4g • saturated fat 2.5g

Variations

You could swap the fresh salmon with 60g/2¼oz tinned salmon, if preferred. Remove any large bones and the skin, then flake into a bowl. Mix in the spice blend and lemon juice. Alternatively, instead of the Cajun spices, you could try an Indian, Chinese or Moroccan spice blend.

Gravadlax Open Sandwich

This Swedish-inspired light lunch comprises nutty-tasting rye bread topped with layers of salad vegetables and omega-3-rich cured salmon. Gravadlax usually comes with a little dill sauce, which is used here as the base for a creamy dressing.

SERVES 2   **PREPARATION** 5 minutes

2 slices rye bread

2 large lettuce leaves

6 slices cucumber

2 slices gravadlax, about 125g/4$\frac{1}{2}$oz in total

1 tbsp dill sauce

1 tbsp low-fat natural bio yogurt

1 tsp lemon juice

1 beetroot in natural juice, sliced

freshly ground black pepper

a little chopped fresh dill, to scatter (optional)

1   Place the bread on a serving plate. Top each slice with a lettuce leaf and 3 slices of cucumber. Arrange the gravadlax on top.

2   Mix together the dill sauce, yogurt and lemon juice and spoon the mixture over the gravadlax. Top with the beetroot, season with pepper, and scatter with a little dill, if using, before serving.

Health Benefits

Salmon is rich in omega-3 fatty acids and a good source of protein, both of which are essential for the health of the skin: vital for cell renewal and help to prevent dryness. By including oily fish regularly in your diet you are also getting valuable amounts of vitamin D – a nutrient that many people are lacking in and one that is important for aiding the absorption of calcium.

Food Facts per Portion

Calories 181kcal • Total Fat 5.1g • saturated fat 0.9g

Variation

An onion or plain bagel would be a suitable alternative to the rye bread. Split the bagel in half and top with the gravadlax, cucumber and lettuce. Spoon over a little of the creamy dill sauce and top with the remaining bagel half.

Tuna & Leek Frittata

○

Choosing tuna tinned in spring water rather than oil will help to keep the levels of fat down in this substantial frittata. Serve with cherry tomatoes and crusty bread.

SERVES 4–6   **PREPARATION** 10 minutes   **COOKING** 12 minutes

1 tbsp sunflower oil

1 large leek, finely sliced

1 courgette/zucchini, sliced

200g/7oz tinned tuna in spring water, drained

6 eggs, lightly beaten

salt and freshly ground black pepper

1   Heat the oil in a medium, ovenproof frying pan and fry the leek and courgette/zucchini for 5 minutes over a low heat until softened. Stir in the tuna, breaking up the fish with a fork but retaining some chunks; make sure that the leek, tuna and courgette/zucchini are evenly spread over the base of the pan.

2   Preheat the grill to medium-high. Season the beaten eggs and pour them carefully over the tuna and leek mixture. Cook over a medium-low heat for 5 minutes or until the eggs are just set and the base of the tortilla (when you lift it with a fish slice) is golden.

3   Put the pan under the preheated grill and cook the top of the tortilla for 2 minutes or until just set and lightly golden. Slide out on to a serving plate and cut into wedges.

Storage

Can be stored in an airtight container in the refrigerator for up to 3 days, then served cold or reheated.

Health Benefits

Although tinned tuna is not as rich in omega-3 as the fresh fish, it still provides useful amounts of this beneficial fatty acid, and is a valuable source of sustaining protein.

Food Facts per Portion (for 6 servings)

Calories 126kcal • Total Fat 7.4g • saturated fat 1.8g

Variation

For a vegetarian version, omit the tuna and replace with 75g/3oz half-fat mature Cheddar cheese.

Spicy Tuna & Bean Tortillas

The beauty of spices is that they give plenty of flavour, negating the need for excessive amounts of oil. Here, smoked paprika is used to give a distinctive smokiness and heat to this rich tuna, bean and tomato sauce.

SERVES 4   **PREPARATION** 10 minutes   **COOKING** 16 minutes

1 tbsp olive oil

2 large garlic cloves, chopped

1 red bell pepper, deseeded and diced

300ml/10½fl oz/1¼ cups sugocassa or passata

1 tsp smoked paprika

1 tsp ground cumin

1 tbsp tomato paste

400g/14oz tinned red kidney beans in water, drained and rinsed

1 tbsp lime juice

200g/7oz tinned tuna in spring water, drained

4 soft wholemeal tortillas

1 small avocado, pitted, peeled and diced

handful fresh coriander/cilantro

salt and freshly ground black pepper

1 Heat the oil in a non-stick saucepan and sauté the garlic and red bell pepper over a medium-low heat for 1 minute until softened.

2 Add the sugocasa, smoked paprika, cumin, tomato paste and kidney beans and cook for 12 minutes until reduced and thickened. Add the lime juice and stir in the tuna, then cook for a further 3 minutes. Season to taste.

3 Meanwhile, warm the tortillas, 2 at a time, in a dry frying pan, turning occasionally until warmed through. Place the tortillas on four plates and spoon the tuna mixture on top. Spoon the avocado on top, scatter with the coriander/cilantro and serve.

Storage

The tuna filling can be stored in an airtight container in the refrigerator for up to 2 days, then served cold or reheated.

Health Benefits

Red bell peppers provide good amounts of the naturally occurring carotenoid pigment lutein. Since this potent antioxidant cannot be made in the body, it is vital that it is provided by the diet. Important for healthy vision, lutein also helps to protect the skin, improving hydration and elasticity.

Food Facts per Portion

Calories 262kcal • Total Fat 6.4g • saturated fat 1.3g

Italian Seafood Salad

This light salad makes a quick and simple summery lunch.

SERVES 4   **PREPARATION** 5 minutes

4 large iceberg lettuce leaves, shredded

400g/14oz mixed cooked seafood

16 cherry tomatoes, halved

Dressing:

2–3 tbsp lemon juice

4 tsp extra-virgin olive oil

1 red chilli, deseeded and finely chopped

1 small garlic clove, finely chopped

salt and freshly ground black pepper

1 Put the lettuce in a shallow serving bowl and spoon over the seafood and tomatoes.

2 Mix together the dressing ingredients. Taste and add more lemon juice, if liked, then season well and spoon over the salad.

Health Benefits

Seafood is a good supplier of copper and zinc, which are crucial for helping the skin to maintain and create collagen and elastin.

Food Facts per Portion

Calories 124kcal • Total Fat 4.6g • saturated fat 0.8g

Prawns/Shrimp with Tomato Salsa

Lentils are low in fat and provide fibre, vitamins and minerals.

SERVES 4   **PREPARATION** 10 minutes

200g/7oz mixed salad leaves

200g/7oz tinned green lentils in water, drained and rinsed

300g/10½oz cooked medium peeled prawns/shrimp

Tomato salsa:

4 tomatoes, deseeded and diced

1 small cucumber, diced

1 red onion, diced

2 tbsp lime juice

½ tsp crushed dried chillies

small handful chopped coriander/cilantro

salt

1 Mix the salsa ingredients together and season with salt to taste.

2 Divide the salad leaves between four plates and top with the lentils and prawns/shrimp. Spoon the salsa over before serving.

Health Benefits

Fresh coriander/cilantro helps to ease indigestion and nausea.

Food Facts per Portion

Calories 156kcal • Total Fat 1.5g • saturated fat 0.3g

Real Prawn/Shrimp Cocktail

Nothing beats a homemade prawn/shrimp cocktail, and this low-fat version of the popular retro dish can be rustled up in a matter of minutes – and that's from scratch. Slices of wholemeal bread are the classic accompaniment, or you could stir the prawn mixture into cold, cooked pasta shells to make a delicious salad.

SERVES 4   **PREPARATION** 10 minutes

2 tbsp light mayonnaise

2 tbsp 0% fat Greek yogurt

2 tbsp tomato ketchup

few drops of Tabasco

350g/12oz large cooked peeled prawns/shrimp

6 large Romaine lettuce leaves, shredded

½ tsp paprika (optional)

salt and freshly ground black pepper

lemon wedges, to serve

1 Mix together the mayonnaise, yogurt, ketchup and Tabasco, and season. Taste and add a few more drops of Tabasco, if liked. Add the prawns/shrimp and turn to coat in the sauce.

2 Arrange the lettuce leaves in four shallow bowls. Spoon the prawn cocktail on top, sprinkle with paprika, if using, and serve with lemon wedges.

Storage

The prawn/shrimp mixture can be stored in an airtight container in the refrigerator for up to 12 hours. Assemble the salad just before you want to serve it.

Health Benefits

Contrary to popular belief, dietary cholesterol found in seafood such as prawns/shrimp is not thought to make a great contribution to increased levels of cholesterol in the blood. For heart health, it is more important to eat foods that are low in saturated fat rather than low in cholesterol.

Food Facts per Portion

Calories 123kcal • Total Fat 3g • saturated fat 0.4g

Garlic & Lemon Squid Linguine

The beauty of squid is that is takes mere minutes to cook – any longer and it becomes tough. Make sure you buy cleaned and prepared squid if you dislike handling seafood or are short of time.

SERVES 4   **PREPARATION** 10 minutes   **COOKING** 14 minutes

300g/10$\frac{1}{2}$oz linguine

550g/1lb 4oz cleaned and prepared squid, sliced into rings

1 tbsp olive oil

4 garlic cloves, chopped

juice and finely grated zest of 1 large lemon

$\frac{1}{2}$ tsp crushed dried chillies

small handful fresh flat-leaf parsley, chopped, to scatter

salt and freshly ground black pepper

1   Cook the pasta in plenty of boiling salted water following the packet instructions. Drain, reserving 4 tablespoons of the water.

2   Meanwhile, rinse and pat dry the squid.

3   Heat the oil in a sauté pan and fry the garlic, lemon zest and crushed dried chillies for 30 seconds over a medium heat. Add the squid to the pan and fry for another 1–2 minutes. Pour in the lemon juice and the reserved pasta water, then season.

4 Toss in the pasta and turn until everything is mixed together. Divide the pasta and squid between four plates and pour over any juices. Scatter with the parsley before serving.

Health Benefits

Squid is a good source of omega-3 fatty acids, which research has shown contribute to the good health of brain tissue as well as the health of the skin and eyes. Poor intake of omega-3 fats has been linked to low moods and depression.

Food Facts per Portion

Calories 391kcal • Total Fat 6g • saturated fat 1g

Variation

Other types of seafood could be used in place of the squid, including prawns/shrimp, mussels, clams or scallops.

Crab Salad with Herb Mayo

The creamy herb dressing complements the richness of the crab in this delicious salad. This would make an excellent light lunch with friends or a starter for a dinner party.

SERVES 4   **PREPARATION** 10 minutes   **COOKING** 2 minutes

4 thick slices wholemeal bread

2 dressed crabs

140g/5oz mixed salad leaves

lemon wedges, to serve

Herb mayo:

3 tbsp light mayonnaise

4 tsp lemon juice

2 tbsp chopped fresh basil

2 tbsp chopped fresh oregano

2 tbsp snipped fresh chives

salt and freshly ground black pepper

1   To make the herb mayo, put all the ingredients plus 2 tablespoons warm water in a blender and process until smooth and creamy; season to taste.

2   Lightly toast the bread, then place on four plates. Scoop the crabmeat out of the shells and pile on top of the pieces of toast.

3   Dollop a spoonful of the herb mayo on top of the crab and
    arrange the salad leaves by the side. Serve with lemon wedges
    for squeezing over.

Health Benefits

Crab is a good source of the mineral chromium, which has been
found to help raise levels of HDL ('good' cholesterol) in the body,
thereby reducing the risk of coronary heart disease.

Food Facts per Portion

Calories 207kcal • Total Fat 8.5g • saturated fat 1.1g

Variation

Use new potatoes as an alternative to the bread. Simply spoon the
crab on top of the salad leaves, and serve with the potatoes and
herb mayonnaise.

Ricotta & Herb Pâté

The herbs and lemon juice add a summery flavour to this light vegetarian pâté, which can also be served as a dip with bread-sticks and vegetable crudités.

SERVES 4   **PREPARATION** 10 minutes

125g/4½oz/heaped ½ cup ricotta cheese

small handful fresh mint

small handful fresh basil

juice of ½ lemon

1 tbsp extra-virgin olive oil

1 tbsp low-fat natural bio yogurt

paprika, to sprinkle (optional)

salt and freshly ground black pepper

4 slices crusty wholemeal toast, to serve

1 Put the ricotta, herbs, lemon juice, olive oil, yogurt and seasoning into a blender, then process until almost smooth and creamy.

2 Spread the pâté on slices of toasted wholemeal bread and sprinkle with paprika, if using.

Storage

The pâté can be stored in an airtight container in the refrigerator for up to 2 days.

Health Benefits

Ricotta is a fresh, soft, unripened cheese that is low in fat yet remains a good source of protein and calcium, which promotes bone and cardiovascular health.

Food Facts per Portion

Calories 137kcal • Total Fat 6.6g • saturated fat 2.7g

Variations

This herb pâté also works well with spices. You could try replacing the mint, basil and paprika with ½ teaspoon smoked paprika, and the juice of 1 lime instead of the lemon. Stir until combined, then scatter over 1 tablespoon chopped fresh coriander before serving. Alternatively, omit the basil and replace with 2 teaspoons cumin seeds, toasted in a dry frying pan for about 2 minutes. Stir them into the ricotta with the mint.

Tofu & Miso Soup

Rich in minerals, miso is made from fermented soya beans and can be found either as a paste or in a dried powdered form ready to be rehydrated with boiling water to make a delicious base for soup. The latter often comes with dried nori flakes for an additional mineral boost.

SERVES 1   **PREPARATION** 10 minutes

55g/2oz vermicelli rice noodles

1 sachet instant miso soup powder

1 small carrot, cut into thin strips

½ small red bell pepper, deseeded and thinly sliced

1 tsp tamari

50g/1¾oz soft tofu, cut into cubes

1 small spring onion/scallion, cut into thin strips

crushed dried chillies and nori flakes, to scatter

1 Prepare the noodles following the packet instructions, then drain. Meanwhile, rehydrate the miso soup powder following the packet instructions.

2 Put the noodles in a bowl with the carrot and red bell pepper, then pour over the hot miso soup and tamari. Add the tofu, and stir, then scatter the spring onion/scallion over the top. Scatter with the crushed dried chillies and nori flakes before serving.

Health Benefits

Studies show that eating miso on a regular basis can boost the immune system and also helps to rid the body of unwanted toxins and break down harmful free radicals.

Food Facts per Portion

Calories 273kcal • Total Fat 2.8g • saturated fat 0.3g

Variations

Slices of cooked chicken, beef or pork can also be added to the miso broth to add extra substance to the soup. Seafood lovers may like to add cooked small prawns or cubes of white fish.

Gazpacho with Avocado Salsa

This classic Spanish soup, sometimes referred to as 'salad in a glass', is packed with antioxidant vitamins. If time allows, this soup benefits from chilling for 2–3 hours. Accompany with slices of sourdough bread.

SERVES 4   **PREPARATION** 30 minutes, plus chilling

2 slices day-old wholemeal bread, crusts removed

900g/2lb vine-ripened tomatoes

1 small cucumber, peeled, deseeded and chopped

1 red bell pepper, deseeded and chopped

2 green chillies, deseeded and sliced

2 garlic cloves, crushed

1 tbsp extra-virgin olive oil

juice of 1½ limes

few drops Tabasco sauce, to taste

salt and freshly ground black pepper

few torn fresh basil leaves, to scatter

8 ice cubes, to serve

Avocado salsa:

1 small ripe avocado, pitted, peeled and diced

juice of ½ lime

5cm/2in piece cucumber, diced

1 red chilli, deseeded and finely chopped

1 Soak the bread in a little water for 5 minutes.

2 Meanwhile, peel the tomatoes: make a shallow cross in the top of each tomato then put in a bowl of very hot water for 1 minute. Peel each tomato, then remove the seeds and chop roughly.

3 Put half of the tomatoes, bread, cucumber, bell pepper, chillies, garlic, oil and lime juice, plus 250ml/9fl oz/1 cup chilled water, in a blender or food processor and blend until combined but still chunky. Pour into a bowl. Repeat with the rest of the ingredients. Add the Tabasco and season to taste, then chill for 2–3 hours.

4 Just before serving, make the avocado salsa: toss the avocado in the lime juice, then combine with the cucumber and chilli.

5 Ladle the soup into bowls, add 2 ice cubes per bowl, and top with a spoonful of salsa. Scatter with basil just before serving.

Storage

Can be stored in an airtight container in the refrigerator for up to 3 days.

Health Benefits

Avocados provide good amounts of vitamin E, folate, potassium, magnesium and also B vitamins. What's more, they contain the super nutrient beta-sitosteral, which helps to lower cholesterol.

Food Facts per Portion

Calories 132kcal • Total Fat 6.4g • saturated fat 1.3g

Spicy Cauliflower Salad

This Indian-spiced warm cauliflower salad is peppered with juicy raisins and toasted almonds. Serve with warm naan bread and a hard-boiled egg, cut in half and placed on top of the salad.

SERVES 4   **PREPARATION** 10 minutes   **COOKING** 10 minutes

350g/12oz cauliflower, cut into small florets

1 tbsp olive oil

2 garlic cloves, crushed

2 tsp cumin seeds

2 tsp garam masala

2 tbsp lemon juice

70g/2^1/$_2$oz/^{1}/$_2$ cup raisins

2 tbsp toasted flaked almonds

small handful fresh coriander/cilantro, to scatter

salt and freshly ground black pepper

1 Steam the cauliflower for 10 minutes or until just tender. Leave to cool slightly.

2 Meanwhile, heat the oil in a frying pan, add the garlic and spices and fry for 1 minute over a gentle heat, stirring frequently. Add the cauliflower, lemon juice and 2 tablespoons water. Turn the cauliflower until it is coated in the spices, then season to taste.

3 Transfer the cauliflower to a serving bowl and scatter over the raisins and almonds. Scatter with the coriander/cilantro before serving.

Storage

Can be stored in an airtight container in the refrigerator for up to 2 days.

Health Benefits

Cauliflower, like other cruciferous vegetables, such as broccoli and cabbage, contains compounds that protect against cancer, particularly of the colon and lung. It also aids the detoxification of the liver by disarming free radicals in the body.

Food Facts per Portion

Calories 149kcal • Total Fat 7.6g • saturated fat 0.9g

Japanese-style Smoked Tofu Salad

Ⓥ ⊙ ⊘ ⊕

Tofu, also known as beancurd, is rich in protein and low in fat. It's also incredibly versatile and comes in various types. This simple salad makes use of smoked tofu, which does not require marinating before use, as well as soft silken tofu, which makes a creamy addition to dressings.

SERVES 4   **PREPARATION** 10 minutes   **COOKING** 5–7 minutes

115g/4oz soba noodles

400g/14oz block smoked tofu, drained

1 tsp sesame seeds

175g/6oz white cabbage, finely shredded

1 large carrot, peeled and finely shredded

4 spring onions/scallions, sliced

2 green chillies, deseeded and finely sliced into rings

Dressing:

2 tsp grated fresh root ginger

2 small garlic cloves, crushed

4 tbsp silken tofu

4 tsp tamari

1 tsp sesame oil

salt and freshly ground black pepper

1   Cook the noodles in plenty of boiling salted water following the
    packet instructions. Drain and refresh under cold running water.

2   Meanwhile, steam the block of tofu for 5 minutes, then cut
    into long, thin slices.

3   While the noodles are cooking and the tofu is steaming, put
    the sesame seeds in a frying pan and dry-fry over a medium
    heat for 2 minutes until lightly golden. Set aside.

4   Put all the ingredients for the dressing plus 4 tablespoons hot
    water into a blender and blend until smooth, then season.

5   Mix together the cabbage, carrot, spring onions/scallions and
    chillies. To serve, arrange the noodles on four plates and top
    with the salad and slices of tofu. Spoon the dressing over and
    sprinkle with the toasted sesame seeds before serving.

Health Benefits

Highly nutritious, tofu is a low-fat, protein-rich food. Recent
research shows that regular intake of soy protein can help to lower
total cholesterol levels by as much as 30 per cent, lower LDL
('bad' cholesterol) levels by as much as 35–40 per cent, reduce
triglyceride levels and possibly even raise levels of HDL ('good'
cholesterol).

Food Facts per Portion

Calories 231kcal • Total Fat 8.3g • saturated fat 0.8g

Spiced Vegetable Couscous

Couscous is a quick and easy grain to cook, but its mild flavour does benefit from being combined with stronger flavours such as herbs and spices. Ras el hanout is a traditional blend of herbs and spices that is used in North African cooking.

SERVES 4   **PREPARATION** 15 minutes   **COOKING** 12 minutes

175g/6oz/scant 1 cup couscous, wholegrain if possible

350ml/12fl oz/scant 1½ cups hot vegetable stock

1 tbsp olive oil, plus extra for brushing

1 onion, sliced

2 courgettes/zucchinis, diced

1 red chilli, deseeded and chopped

2 garlic cloves

1 heaped tbsp ras el hanout

juice of ½ lemon

handful fresh coriander/cilantro, chopped

handful fresh mint, chopped

100g/3½oz light halloumi cheese, drained, patted dry and sliced into 4

salt and freshly ground black pepper

1 Put the couscous in a large bowl and pour the vegetable stock over; the liquid should cover the couscous. Stir, then cover and leave for 5 minutes until the couscous has absorbed the stock. Fluff up the grains with a fork.

2 Meanwhile, heat the oil in a frying pan and fry the onion for 5 minutes, stirring occasionally, until softened. Next, add the courgettes/zucchinis, chilli and garlic and stir until combined, then cook for another 3 minutes until light golden. Finally, add the ras el hanout and cook for a further 30 seconds.

3 Remove the pan from the heat and tip the vegetables and lemon juice into the couscous; stir until the grains are coated in the spice mixture. Season the couscous to taste and stir in the coriander/cilantro and mint, reserving a little to scatter.

4 Brush the halloumi slices on one side with oil. Heat a griddle pan until hot. Put the halloumi in the pan, oiled side down, and cook for about $1\frac{1}{2}$ minutes until golden. Brush the tops with oil and turn over; cook for another $1\frac{1}{2}$ minutes.

5 Serve the spiced couscous topped with the halloumi and scattered with the reserved herbs.

Storage

The spiced couscous can be stored in an airtight container in the refrigerator for up to 2 days. Cook the halloumi at the last minute.

Health Benefits

Chillies are richer in vitamin C than an orange and also stimulate the release of endorphins. They are also an effective decongestant.

Food Facts per Portion

Calories 200kcal • Total Fat 6.9g • saturated fat 0.3g

Mediterranean Tortilla Parcel

There is no need to cut out dairy products altogether in a low-fat diet, especially since they are a good source of calcium and protein. However, moderation is the key and it is a good idea to seek out low-fat versions when shopping, such as the light mozzarella cheese used here .

SERVES 1   **PREPARATION** 5 minutes   **COOKING** 4 minutes

---

1 soft wholemeal tortilla

1 slice light mozzarella cheese, about 25g/1oz

1 tomato, halved, deseeded and sliced

5 large fresh basil leaves

1 tsp olive oil

salt and freshly ground black pepper

1   Put the tortilla in a dry frying pan and heat gently until slightly warm and pliable. Remove from the pan and place on a work surface. Put the mozzarella in the centre, top with the tomato and basil and season. Fold in the edges of the tortilla to make a square parcel.

2   Heat a non-stick frying pan and brush with the oil. Put the parcel seam-side down in the frying pan. Cook for 3–4 minutes over a medium-low heat, turning once, until golden, then serve.

Health Benefits

When wheat is refined, it loses a staggering 80 per cent of its nutrients, which explains why it's best to opt for wholegrain foods whenever possible. As well as providing soluble fibre (the type that keeps you regular), wholegrain flour is a good source of vitamins E and B and the minerals selenium, iron and zinc.

Food Facts per Portion

Calories 162kcal • Total Fat 7.2g • saturated fat 0.5g

Variations

Try light halloumi or a reduced-fat Cheddar cheese instead of the mozzarella. A spoonful of onion chutney works well with the latter.

Eggs Florentine

Ⓥ Ⓞ Ⓙ Ⓖ Ⓢ

A perfect family light lunch: the combination of eggs and spinach makes a nutritious meal, and the toast makes it filling, too. The tomatoes are a slight departure from the classic dish, but they do add a nutritional boost and also help to keep the dish moist.

SERVES 4   **PREPARATION** 15 minutes   **COOKING** 17 minutes

600g/1lb 5oz/6½ cups spinach, tough stalks removed, rinsed well

4 eggs

2 tomatoes, halved, deseeded and sliced

2 tbsp virtually fat-free fromage frais

40g/1½oz/scant ½ cup half-fat strong Cheddar cheese, grated

salt and freshly ground black pepper

4 slices wholegrain toast, to serve

1 Preheat the oven to 190°C/375°F/Gas 5. Steam the spinach for about 2 minutes until wilted and tender. Drain, then press out any excess water using the back of a spoon.

2 Spoon the spinach into an ovenproof dish. Make 4 holes in the spinach mixture, and break the eggs into the dips.

3 Arrange the tomato slices around the eggs. Put a dollop of fromage frais on each egg, then scatter the top of the whole dish with the Cheddar. Bake in the preheated oven for 15 minutes or until the eggs are just set and the cheese has melted.

4 Place a slice of toast on each plate and top with a serving of egg, tomato and spinach. Season to taste before serving.

Health Benefits

Opt for strong versions of low-fat cheese, as you will need to use less. As the term suggests, these cheeses have half, or less, the fat content of standard cheese. Moisture and protein levels are slightly higher than those in the comparable whole-milk cheese to compensate for the loss of fat. Consequently, calcium levels are also slightly higher.

Food Facts per Portion

Calories 214kcal • Total Fat 9.1g • saturated fat 2.9g

Provençal Pizza

This makes one large pizza – perfect for sharing as part of a light meal or a simple party dish. You could vary the topping according to taste, but char-grilled artichoke hearts, aubergines and courgettes/zucchinis would all make suitable additions.

SERVES 4

PREPARATION 20 minutes, plus rising   **COOKING** 12–15 minutes

1 tsp instant dried yeast

225g/8oz/scant 2 cups strong plain flour, plus extra for dusting

1 tsp salt

1 tsp olive oil

Topping:

2 tsp olive oil

200ml/7fl oz/generous ¾ cup passata

2 tsp tomato paste

1 tsp dried oregano

20 black olives

2 tbsp capers in a jar, drained and rinsed

handful torn fresh basil

salt and freshly ground black pepper

1 Mix the yeast with 2 tablespoons lukewarm water and
1 tablespoon of the flour in a bowl; set aside for 15 minutes.

2 Sift the remaining flour and salt into a mixing bowl. Make a well
in the centre and add the oil, yeast mixture and 100ml/3½fl oz/
scant ½ cup lukewarm water, then mix to make a soft dough.
If the dough appears dry, stir in another 1 tablespoon water.

3 Turn the dough out on to a work surface dusted with flour.
Knead the dough for 10 minutes until smooth and silky, and form
into a ball. Put the dough in a clean bowl, cover with a cloth
and leave in a warm place for 1½ hours until doubled in size.

4 Preheat the oven to 220°C/425°F/Gas 7. Punch the dough with
your knuckles to release the air, then tip it out onto the floured
surface and knead for 2 minutes. Roll out into a 35 x 25cm/
14 x 10in rectangle and put on a large floured baking sheet.

5 Mix together the olive oil, passata, tomato paste and oregano,
and season to taste, then spread the tomato sauce thinly over
the base. Arrange the olives and capers over the sauce and
bake in the preheated oven for 12–15 minutes until the base is
golden and crisp. Scatter over the basil leaves before serving.

Health Benefits

Packed with 'super nutrients', tomatoes contain the red pigment lycopene, which has been found to aid both mental and physical function if consumed regularly. The antioxidant lutein is also found in significant amounts.

Food Facts per Portion

Calories 235kcal • Total Fat 3.9g • saturated fat 0.6g

Variation

Instead of a cooked topping, you could try this southern Italian version, which makes a quick and summery light meal. Top the cooked pizza base with a large handful of rocket leaves and diced deseeded tomatoes. Season well and scatter over a few basil leaves and drizzle with a little extra-virgin olive oil. You could also add some cubes of light mozzarella cheese.

Main Meals

Cooking from scratch makes it so much easier to control the amount of fat you eat, and it also relieves the burden – and boredom – of having to scrutinize labels on ready-made processed foods. This chapter dispels the myth that low-fat cooking is dull with a collection of recipes that takes its inspiration from all corners of the world, including Vietnamese Beef Broth, Turkey & Mango Stir-fry, Moules Marinière, Greek Salad, Mixed Bean & Vegetable Tagine and Thai Green Vegetable Curry.

However, low-fat cooking is not just about how much fat you eat but also about what type of fat it is, and this chapter makes the most of beneficial omega-3 fats in dishes such as Salmon in Black Bean Sauce, Steamed Trout Parcels and Smoked Trout Salad with Dill Dressing.

Low-fat cooking techniques, such as grilling, steaming and stir-frying, are also adopted. Although these methods use little or no extra oil, the flavour of the dish is not affected in a detrimental way. In addition, by simply removing the skin on a chicken breast, for example, you can reduce its saturated fat content by one-third – it's as easy as that!

Pork with Minty Pea Purée

The minty pea purée makes a great accompaniment to meat and also works well with grilled fish. Serve this dish with baked potatoes and steamed broccoli.

SERVES 4   **PREPARATION** 10 minutes   **COOKING** 6 minutes

4 lean pork fillets, about 140g/5oz each

2 tsp olive oil

Minty pea purée:

400g/14oz/3½ cups frozen peas

1 tbsp skimmed milk

3–4 tbsp vegetable stock

1 tbsp half-fat crème fraîche

4 tbsp chopped fresh mint

salt and freshly ground black pepper

1 Preheat the grill to high. Brush each side of the pork with oil and grill for about 3 minutes on each side until browned and cooked.

2 Meanwhile, cook the peas until tender. Drain and transfer to a blender with the milk and 3 tablespoons of the stock, and blend until smooth. Pour the purée into a saucepan and stir in the crème fraîche and mint, then heat through gently; season to taste. If the purée appears too thick, add the remaining stock.

3 Serve the pork fillets with the minty pea purée.

Storage

The pea purée can be stored in an airtight container in the refrigerator for up to 1 day, then reheated gently.

Health Benefits

As pulses, peas contain significant amounts of protein, carbohydrate and fibre and very little fat. A single serving of peas provides as much vitamin C as two large apples and more fibre than a slice of wholemeal bread. Peas also provide vitamin A, vitamin C, folate, thiamine (B1), iron and phosphorus.

Food Facts per Portion

Calories 327kcal • Total Fat 8.7g • saturated fat 2.9g

Pork & Vegetable Ramen

This Japanese broth makes a nutritious and sustaining complete
meal thanks to its combination of pork, noodles and vegetables.
Soba noodles are made of buckwheat, and therefore gluten-free,
but sometimes wheat is added to the recipe, which means
coeliacs should always check the label before buying them.

SERVES 4   **PREPARATION** 15 minutes   **COOKING** 14 minutes

250g/9oz soba noodles

300g/10½ oz lean pork loin, thickly sliced

2 tsp sunflower oil

1.25 litres/44fl oz/5 cups vegetable stock

2.5cm/1in piece fresh root ginger, peeled and cut into fine
matchsticks

3 tbsp brown rice miso paste

4 tbsp Chinese cooking wine or dry sherry

3 tbsp soy sauce

1 large carrot, sliced into fine matchsticks

4 heads pak choi/bok choy, sliced lengthways

4 spring onions/scallions, cut on the diagonal

100g/3½ oz/1 cup beansprouts

½ tsp crushed dried chillies

handful fresh coriander/cilantro, chopped

1 Cook the noodles following the packet instructions, then drain
   and refresh under cold running water. Put the noodles in a bowl
   and cover with cold water; set aside.

2 Meanwhile, brush the pork with the oil. Heat a griddle pan
   over a high heat, then cook the pork for 2–3 minutes on each
   side until the meat is browned and just cooked. Remove the
   pan from the heat and set aside.

3 Heat the stock in a large saucepan and stir in the ginger, miso
   paste, cooking wine and soy sauce. Bring to the boil, then
   reduce the heat and simmer, half-covered, for 5 minutes.

4 Add the carrot and pak choi/bok choy and half the spring
   onions/scallions, then simmer for another 3 minutes, adding
   the beansprouts at the end of the cooking time.

5 Drain the noodles and divide between four bowls. Add the
   vegetables to the bowls, then pour the stock over the top.

6 Arrange the slices of cooked pork on top, then scatter with
   the crushed dried chillies, coriander/cilantro and the
   remaining spring onions/scallions.

Health Benefits

Buckwheat is not a true cereal as it is not part of the grass family; however, it is gluten free and is a good source of calcium as well as iron and B vitamins. It has also been found to act as a prebiotic, encouraging the growth of beneficial bacteria in the digestive tract.

Food Facts per Portion

Calories 477kcal • Total Fat 11.9g • saturated fat 1.9g

Variations

Experiment with different types of noodle: in place of the soba you could try rice noodles, egg noodles or udon noodles. Beef or chicken could also be used instead of the pork. Or why not try prawns or cubes of white fish? Vegetarians may like to replace the pork with a hard-boiled egg, halved, or an omelette cut into thin strips.

Vietnamese Beef Broth

Chillies, ginger, star anise and lemongrass produce a light, fragrant stock and a flavourful base to this main-meal noodle, beef and vegetable soup.

SERVES 4   **PREPARATION** 15 minutes   **COOKING** 25 minutes

1.25 litres/44fl oz/5 cups vegetable stock

2 tbsp fish sauce

2 star anise

3 bird's eye chillies, deseeded and halved

2 lemongrass stalks, peeled and crushed

5cm/2in piece fresh root ginger, peeled and sliced

3 garlic cloves, sliced

3 kaffir lime leaves

250g/9oz medium rice noodles

300g/10½oz lean beef fillet, thinly sliced into ribbons

150g/5½oz fine green beans

150g/5½oz mangetout

large handful beansprouts

juice of 1 large lime

1 tbsp soy sauce

4 spring onions/scallions, finely sliced on the diagonal

handful fresh coriander/cilantro, chopped

1 Put the stock, fish sauce, star anise, chillies, lemongrass, ginger, garlic and lime leaves in a large saucepan. Bring to the boil, then reduce the heat and simmer, covered, for 15 minutes.

2 Meanwhile, cook the rice noodles following the packet instructions, then drain and refresh under cold running water. Put the noodles in a bowl and cover with cold water; set aside.

3 Strain the stock, discard the solids and return the flavoured stock to the saucepan. Add the beef and cook for 2 minutes, then add the green beans and mangetout and cook for a further 4 minutes. Stir in the beansprouts, lime juice, soy sauce, spring onions/scallions and half the coriander/cilantro and heat through briefly.

4 Divide the noodles between four bowls and spoon the beef broth over them. Scatter the remaining coriander/cilantro over the top.

Storage

The beef broth can be made up to 2 days in advance and reheated when required. Cook the noodles just before serving and divide them between four bowls as in step 4.

Health Benefits

Historically, ginger has been recognized for its calmative properties, particularly of the digestive system. It can be effective in relieving nausea, vomiting and travel sickness. Additionally, ginger works as an antioxidant and is an effective anti-inflammatory, painkiller and may even have a preventative effect on certain cancers.

Food Facts per Portion

Calories 366kcal • Total Fat 5.3g • saturated fat 2.2g

Variation

Just by changing the spices in this broth you can create a dish of different origin, so from Vietnam we travel to China. Simply omit the fish sauce, lemongrass and kaffir lime leaves and add 3 tablespoons Chinese cooking wine or dry sherry and 1 teaspoon Chinese five-spice in step 1. Additionally, increase the quantity of soy sauce to 2 tablespoons. You can also swap the beef for pork or chicken, and for a vegetarian version include 250g/9oz tofu, cut into cubes.

Beef & Mushroom Stir-fry

The secret to a successful stir-fry is organization: make sure the vegetables are prepared and that other ingredients are weighed and measured before you start to cook, and everything will run smoothly. Serve the stir-fry with egg noodles.

SERVES 4 **PREPARATION** 15 minutes **COOKING** 5 minutes

1 tbsp sunflower oil

400g/14oz lean beef fillet, cut into thin strips

3 garlic cloves, finely chopped

5cm/2in piece fresh root ginger, peeled and finely chopped

1 tsp Sichuan peppercorns, crushed

200g/7oz chestnut mushrooms, sliced

1 large red bell pepper, deseeded and sliced

4 spring onions/scallions, sliced on the diagonal

3 tbsp soy sauce

4 tbsp fresh orange juice

1   Heat the oil in a wok or large frying pan. Add the beef and stir-fry over a medium heat for 1 minute until browned all over. Using a slotted spoon, remove the beef from the wok and set aside.

2   Put the garlic, ginger and Sichuan peppercorns into the wok and stir-fry for 30 seconds. Add the mushrooms, bell pepper and half the spring onions/scallions and stir-fry for 2–3 minutes.

3 Return the beef to the wok with the soy sauce and orange juice
and stir-fry for another minute. Scatter with the remaining
spring onions/scallions before serving.

Health Benefits

Mushrooms provide selenium – an antioxidant that works in
tandem with vitamin E to protect cells from the damaging effects
of free radicals. Potassium, a mineral that helps to reduce high
blood pressure, is also found in useful amounts, as are iron, niacin
and riboflavin.

Food Facts per Portion

Calories 196kcal • Total Fat 9.3g • saturated fat 3.2g

Japanese-style Beef Salad

If you have any cooked beef left over from the Sunday roast, this simple yet delicious salad is the perfect way to use it up. Chicken, prawns/shrimp or pork would all make good alternatives to the beef, if wanted. Serve with rice noodles or soba noodles.

SERVES 4   **COOKING** 2 minutes   **PREPARATION** 15 minutes

large handful baby spinach leaves

225g/8oz radishes, thinly sliced into rounds

100g/3½ oz mangetout, diagonally sliced

1 carrot, cut into thin strips

handful sprouted mixed beans

300g/10½ oz cooked beef, thinly sliced

3 spring onions/scallions, sliced into thin strips

2 tsp sesame seeds

Dressing:

1 tbsp sunflower oil

½ tsp toasted sesame oil

1 tbsp rice vinegar

1 tbsp light soy sauce

2.5cm/1in piece fresh root ginger, peeled and grated

1 To make the dressing, mix together the sunflower oil, toasted sesame oil, rice vinegar and soy sauce in a bowl. Squeeze the grated ginger in your hand to extract the juice and add to the rest of the dressing ingredients; stir until combined.

2 Arrange the spinach, radishes, mangetout, carrot and sprouted beans on a serving plate. Top with the beef and spring onions/ scallions, then spoon the dressing over the salad.

3 Put the sesame seeds in a dry frying pan and cook for 2 minutes over a medium-low heat until slightly golden. Sprinkle over the salad before serving.

Storage

The dressing can be stored in an airtight jar in the refrigerator for up to 1 week.

Health Benefits

Radishes are a member of the cruciferous family of vegetables, along with broccoli, cabbage, cauliflower and turnips. These vegetables are known for their high levels of phytochemicals, or plant compounds, which are said to provide an anti-carcinogenic cocktail, believed to play a crucial role in fighting disease by stimulating the body's defence mechanism.

Food Facts per Portion

Calories 214kcal • Total Fat 11g • saturated fat 3.4g

Thai Chicken Broth

Thai soups should be a combination of hot, sour and salty flavours. This soup contains a minimal amount of fat but, nevertheless, makes a filling and nutritious complete meal.

SERVES 4   **PREPARATION** 15 minutes   **COOKING** 25 minutes

1.5 litres/52fl oz/6 cups chicken stock

2 lemongrass stalks

6 slices fresh root ginger, plus 4 slices, peeled and cut
    into matchsticks

4 kaffir lime leaves

2 garlic cloves, thinly sliced

2 tbsp fish sauce

400g/14oz skinless boneless chicken breasts

115g/4oz/heaped 1 cup baby spinach leaves

1 tbsp rice vinegar

juice of 1 lime

2 red chillies, finely chopped

600g/1lb 5oz ready-cooked rice noodles

small handful fresh coriander/cilantro

salt and freshly ground black pepper

1 Put the stock, lemongrass, 6 ginger slices, kaffir lime leaves, garlic and fish sauce into a large saucepan. Add the chicken breasts and bring to the boil, then reduce the heat and simmer, half-covered, for about 20 minutes until the chicken is cooked through and there is no trace of pink in the centre.

2 Scoop out the chicken using a slotted spoon and set aside. Strain the stock, discarding the solids, and return the stock to the pan.

3 Add the ginger matchsticks to the pan with the spinach, rice vinegar, lime juice and chillies. Bring to the boil, then reduce the heat and simmer, half-covered, for 2–3 minutes until the spinach is cooked. Add the noodles and heat through.

4 Slice the chicken into strips and divide between four bowls; pour the noodles, spinach and stock over them. Season and scatter with coriander/cilantro before serving.

Health Benefits

Spinach is a good source of cancer-fighting antioxidants, particularly beta carotene. It is also rich in fibre, which helps to lower levels of LDL (harmful cholesterol) in the body, reducing the risk of heart disease and strokes.

Food Facts per Portion

Calories 257kcal • Total Fat 3.2g • saturated fat 0.6g

Chicken Tikka

The lightly spiced yogurt marinade helps to keep the chicken moist and succulent during cooking. Serve with warm naan bread and a mint raita.

SERVES 4

PREPARATION 15 minutes, plus marinating   **COOKING** 12–20 minutes

4 skinless boneless chicken breasts, about 150g/5¹/₂oz each

Marinade:

2 garlic cloves, crushed

2.5cm/1in piece fresh root ginger, peeled and grated

2 tbsp lemon juice

2 tbsp tikka spice blend

¹/₂ tsp hot chilli powder

1 tsp paprika

185ml/6fl oz/³/₄ cup low-fat natural bio yogurt

salt

To serve:

6 large, crisp salad leaves, shredded

1 small cucumber, thickly sliced

4 tomatoes, quartered

4 lemon wedges

1 Make 3 diagonal cuts across each chicken breast.

2 Mix together all the ingredients for the marinade in a shallow dish. Add the chicken and turn to coat in the marinade. Leave to marinate for 1 hour or overnight, if possible.

3 Preheat the grill to high. Put the chicken on the grill pan, spoon over any surplus marinade and grill for 6–10 minutes, depending on the thickness of the breasts. Turn over and spoon a little more marinade over each breast, then cook for a further 6–10 minutes until cooked through with no trace of pink in the centre.

4 Serve the chicken accompanied by the lettuce, cucumber and tomatoes, with lemon wedges for squeezing over.

Health Benefits

Garlic really does deserve the title 'superfood', with its impressively long list of health benefits. Numerous studies have linked the regular consumption of garlic with an ability to reduce the risk of heart disease and strokes. This is due to the presence of sulphur compounds, vitamin C, vitamin B6, manganese and selenium.

Food Facts per Portion

Calories 204kcal • Total Fat 2.6g • saturated fat 0.8g

Spanish Chicken Casserole

The smoked paprika gives this casserole a characteristically distinctive Spanish flavour and a warming spicy heat. Serve with brown rice and steamed green beans.

SERVES 4   **PREPARATION** 15 minutes   **COOKING** 40–45 minutes

4 skinless boneless chicken breasts, about 150g/5½oz each, cut into 2.5cm/1in cubes

plain flour, for dusting

1 tbsp olive oil

1 large red onion, sliced

1 large orange bell pepper, deseeded and sliced

3 large garlic cloves, chopped

150ml/5fl oz/scant ⅔ cup dry sherry

100ml/3½fl oz/scant ½ cup chicken stock

1 bay leaf

juice and finely grated zest of 1 orange

1 tsp smoked paprika

1 tsp Worcestershire sauce

40g/1½oz black olives

salt and freshly ground black pepper

1   Dust the chicken pieces in seasoned flour. Heat the oil in a large
    casserole dish, add the chicken and sauté for about 5 minutes
    until browned all over. Remove from the pan and set aside.

2   Add the onion to the pan and sauté, covered, for 5 minutes.
    Next, add the orange bell pepper and garlic, then cook for
    another 3 minutes before returning the chicken to the pan.

3   Pour in the sherry and bring to the boil, then cook for about
    3 minutes or until the sherry has reduced and there is no
    aroma of alcohol.

4   Stir in the remaining ingredients and return to the boil, then
    reduce the heat and simmer, half-covered, for 20–25 minutes
    until the chicken is cooked and the sauce has reduced.

Storage

Can be stored in an airtight container in the refrigerator for up to
1 day, then reheated.

Health Benefits

Skinless chicken is very low in fat when compared with other meats
and is a good source of the trace mineral selenium, which supports
the immune system. It is also a good source of the amino acid
tryptophan, which is vital for the production of the 'feel-good' brain
chemical serotonin.

Food Facts per Portion

Calories 329kcal • Total Fat 7.6g • saturated fat 1.5g

Coriander Chicken with Lemon Quinoa

Quinoa benefits from being combined with stronger flavourings, such as the lemon and thyme used here.

SERVES 4   **PREPARATION** 20 minutes   **COOKING** 25 minutes

2 tbsp coriander seeds, crushed

1 tsp paprika

4 skinless boneless chicken breasts, about 150g/5$\frac{1}{2}$oz each

2 tsp olive oil

Lemon quinoa:

200g/7oz/1 cup quinoa

about 600ml/20fl oz/2$\frac{1}{2}$ cups hot vegetable stock

juice and finely grated zest of 2 lemons

5 tbsp fresh thyme leaves

salt and freshly ground black pepper

1 Preheat the grill to high. Put the quinoa in a medium saucepan and pour in the stock until it is about 1cm/$\frac{1}{2}$in above the level of the quinoa. Bring to the boil, then reduce the heat and simmer, covered, for about 10 minutes until the stock has been absorbed and the quinoa is tender. Remove from the heat and leave the quinoa to stand for 5 minutes, then fluff up with a fork.

2 While the quinoa is cooking, mix together the coriander and paprika on a plate. Brush both sides of each chicken breast with the oil and press the top of the chicken into the spice mix.

3 Place the chicken on the grill rack, spice-side up first, and cook under the preheated grill for 6–8 minutes, turning halfway, depending on the thickness of the breasts, until cooked through with no trace of pink in the centre.

4 Put the cooked quinoa in a bowl and stir in the lemon juice and zest and the thyme, then season to taste.

5 Divide the quinoa between four plates and top with the chicken.

Storage
The quinoa can be served cold; store, covered, in the refrigerator for up to 2 days, then return to room temperature before serving.

Health Benefits
The 'superfood' quinoa is unusual for a plant food in that it is what is known as a complete protein, since it contains all nine essential amino acids. Lysine is an amino acid that is essential for tissue repair and maintenance. Quinoa is also a good source of magnesium and riboflavin, both of which play a valuable role in reducing the likelihood of migraines and headaches.

Food Facts per Portion
Calories 402kcal • Total Fat 7.9g • saturated fat 1.4g

Poached Chicken with Spring Vegetables

Poaching is a simple and excellent method of cooking without the need for oil, but it is important to add flavourings to the cooking liquid to impart flavour to whatever you are cooking. Serve the chicken with new potatoes in their skin.

SERVES 4   **PREPARATION** 15 minutes   **COOKING** 20–25 minutes

4 skinless boneless chicken breasts, about 150g/5½oz each

200ml/7fl oz/generous ¾ cup dry white wine

2 onions, quartered

1 celery stalk, thickly sliced

2 bay leaves

2 fresh rosemary sprigs

350g/12oz fine green beans

12 asparagus spears, trimmed

2 courgettes/zucchinis, halved and sliced lengthways

squeeze of fresh lemon juice

4 tbsp light pesto

salt and freshly ground black pepper

1   Put the chicken in a large sauté pan with the wine, onions, celery, bay leaves and rosemary. Add enough water to just cover the chicken. Bring to the boil, then reduce the heat and simmer, half-covered, for about 15–20 minutes until the chicken is cooked and there is no trace of pink in the centre.

2   Meanwhile, steam the green beans for 6–7 minutes, adding the asparagus and courgettes/zucchinis in the final 4 minutes and cooking until just tender.

3   Remove the chicken from the cooking liquid and slice. Arrange the vegetables in four large, shallow bowls and top with the chicken. Squeeze over a little lemon juice, season, and top with a spoonful of pesto before serving.

Health Benefits

Fresh rosemary is reputed to boost circulation, digestion and the immune system. There is also the widespread belief that the herb improves memory and concentration by stimulating an increase of blood flow to the brain.

Food Facts per Portion

Calories 352kcal • Total Fat 9.2g • saturated fat 1g

Chicken Escalopes with Mango Salsa

A fruity salsa is a great way of adding bundles of flavour to a dish without the need for lots of oil or a rich creamy sauce. Mangoes add a wonderful, luxuriously exotic flavour to the salsa, but you could also use pineapple or papaya. Serve with a baked potato and green salad.

SERVES 4   **PREPARATION** 10 minutes   **COOKING** 6–8 minutes

4 skinless boneless chicken breasts, about 150g/5½oz each

1 tsp lemon juice

2 tsp olive oil

salt and freshly ground black pepper

Mango salsa:

1 mango, peeled

1 small red onion, finely diced

juice of 1 lime, plus wedges to serve

1 red chilli, deseeded and finely chopped

4 tbsp torn fresh basil

1   Put the chicken breasts between 2 sheets of cling film and flatten them with a rolling pin. Squeeze over a little lemon juice and season.

2 Heat a griddle pan until hot and brush the chicken with the oil. Char-grill the chicken for about 3–4 minutes on each side, depending on the thickness of the breasts, until cooked through with no trace of pink in the centre.

3 Meanwhile, to make the salsa, slice the mango flesh away from the stone and cut into small dice. Put the mango and any juices in a bowl with the red onion, lime juice, chilli and basil. Season with salt and stir to combine.

4 Serve the chicken with the mango salsa spooned over the top and a wedge of fresh lime by the side.

Storage

The salsa can be stored in the refrigerator in an airtight container for up to 2 days.

Health Benefits

It comes as no surprise that mango is rich in the antioxidant beta carotene, thanks to its luscious orange-coloured flesh. The fruit also provides rich amounts of vitamin C and potassium.

Food Facts per Portion

Calories 273kcal · Total Fat 5.9g · saturated fat 1.3g

Chicken with Pico de Gallo

In Mexico, pico de gallo is the general name given to a fresh condiment or salsa, which can vary in its ingredients, though it is also the name of a spice mix that can be sprinkled over fruit. Here, it is used as an accompaniment to grilled chicken. Serve the chicken and pico de gallo in warm taco shells with a spoonful of reduced-fat guacamole.

SERVES 4   **PREPARATION** 15 minutes   **COOKING** 6–8 minutes

4 skinless boneless chicken breasts, about 150g/5½oz each

2 tsp olive oil

1 tsp ground cumin

Pico de gallo:

8 radishes, finely chopped

6 vine-ripened tomatoes, deseeded and chopped

1 small red onion, finely chopped

2 green chillies, deseeded and finely chopped

juice of 1 lime

handful fresh coriander/cilantro

salt and freshly ground black pepper

1   Preheat the grill to high. Put the chicken breasts between
    2 sheets of cling film and flatten with a rolling pin.

2   Lightly brush the chicken breasts with the oil, then rub in the
    cumin. Cook under the preheated grill for about 3–4 minutes
    on each side, depending on the thickness of the breasts, until
    cooked through with no trace of pink in the centre.

3   While the chicken is cooking, make the pico de gallo by mixing
    all the ingredients together and seasoning to taste. Serve with
    the grilled chicken.

Storage

The pico de gallo can be stored in an airtight container in the
refrigerator for up to 2 days.

Health Benefits

Eating half an onion a day has been found to thin the blood, reduce
LDL (harmful cholesterol) and raise levels of HDL (beneficial cholesterol) by about 30 per cent, reducing the risk of heart disease
and strokes. Onions also have antibacterial and antiviral properties.

Food Facts per Portion

Calories 262kcal • Total Fat 5.3g • saturated fat 1.2g

Turkey & Mango Stir-fry

A stir-fry is the perfect low-fat fast meal, and can be infinitely varied depending on what ingredients and flavourings you have to hand. This is typically Thai in style, with its combination of sweet, sour, hot and salty flavours.

SERVES 4   **PREPARATION** 20 minutes   **COOKING** 8 minutes

250g/9oz wholemeal noodles

1 tbsp sunflower oil

450g/1lb skinless turkey breasts, cut into thin strips

2 large garlic cloves, chopped

2 bird's eye chillies, deseeded and chopped

juice of 1 lime

2 tbsp fish sauce

4 spring onions/scallions, sliced on the diagonal

4 pak choi/bok choy, sliced

300g/10½oz mango, sliced

handful fresh coriander/cilantro, to scatter

1 Cook the noodles following the packet instructions, then drain and refresh under cold running water. Set aside.

2 Meanwhile, heat the oil in a wok. When hot, add the turkey and stir-fry for 5 minutes or until cooked; transfer to a plate and keep warm.

3 Add the garlic, chillies, lime juice, fish sauce, spring onions/ scallions and pak choi/bok choy to the wok and stir-fry for a further 2 minutes.

4 Return the turkey to the wok with the mango; stir to combine and heat through. Scatter with the coriander/cilantro leaves before serving with the noodles.

Health Benefits

Turkey, alongside chicken, has become a popular low-fat meat. Without its skin, turkey contains only 1g fat per 25g/1oz meat. It is also a good source of B vitamins, which are essential for energy production and the nervous system, and promote growth and boost mental ability.

Food Facts per Portion

Calories 483kcal • Total Fat 5.4g • saturated fat 1.1g

Char-grilled Venison with Berry Sauce

Venison is an exceptionally lean meat, and so the steaks should be cooked briefly to prevent them drying out. This dish is very quick and easy to make and can be served with steamed green beans and mash.

SERVES 4   **PREPARATION** 15 minutes   **COOKING** 10 minutes

4 venison steaks, about 150g/5¹/₂oz each, trimmed of any fat

2 tsp olive oil

salt and freshly ground black pepper

Berry sauce:

200g/7oz/heaped 1 cup frozen mixed berries, defrosted

2 apples, peeled, cored and diced

1 star anise

¹/₂ tsp sugar, or to taste

1   To make the berry sauce, put all the ingredients and 3 tablespoons water in a saucepan. Bring to a fast boil, then reduce the heat and simmer, covered, for 8 minutes until the apple is tender. Remove the star anise and transfer to a blender. Purée the fruit until smooth, then press the pulp through a sieve to remove any seeds.

2 Meanwhile, preheat the grill to high. Brush the venison lightly with the oil, then season. Grill the venison for 3–4 minutes on each side, depending on the thickness of the steaks, or until cooked to your liking. Serve the venison with the berry sauce (warmed through, if preferred).

Storage

The berry sauce will keep stored in an airtight container in the refrigerator for up to 5 days or the freezer for up to 3 months.

Health Benefits

A 150g/5½oz venison steak provides around one-third of the daily requirement for iron, but is lower in calories and fat than beef – its iron-rich counterpart. Iron is key to energy production and metabolism. B vitamins are also found in significant amounts, particularly B12, which is essential for the formation of red blood cells, maintaining a healthy nervous system and for energy levels.

Food Facts per Portion

Calories 198kcal · Total Fat 4g · saturated fat 1.4g

Fish Tikka Brochettes

These kebabs are marinated in a lightly spiced yogurt marinade, which keeps the fish moist during cooking as well as adding flavour. Serve with brown rice and a tomato and red onion salad.

SERVES 4

PREPARATION 20 minutes, plus marinating   **COOKING** 5–7 minutes

700g/1lb 9 oz firm, thick, white fish fillets, skinned and cut into
    2.5cm/1in cubes

2 tsp sunflower oil

2 mild green chillies, deseeded and finely chopped

lime wedges, to serve

Marinade:

2 tsp ground cumin

2 tsp ground coriander

2 tsp garam masala

2 large garlic cloves, crushed

$\frac{1}{2}$ tsp chilli powder

125ml/4fl oz/$\frac{1}{2}$ cup low-fat natural bio yogurt

salt

1 Mix together all the ingredients for the marinade in a shallow dish. Season with salt. Add the cubes of fish, turning them carefully until coated in the marinade. Cover with cling film and leave to marinate for 30 minutes.

2 Preheat the grill to medium-high and line the grill pan with foil. Brush the foil with half the oil.

3 Thread the cubes of fish onto 8 metal skewers and brush with the oil, then cook under the preheated grill for about 5–7 minutes, turning occasionally, until cooked. Scatter over the green chillies and serve with the lime wedges for squeezing over.

Health Benefits

Low in fat and high in protein, white fish ticks all the right boxes when it comes to a low-fat diet. It is also a good source of B vitamins, zinc and selenium, which are vital for a healthy nervous system and mental processing.

Food Facts per Portion

Calories 177kcal • Total Fat 3.8g • saturated fat 0.6g

Spicy Fish & Chickpea Soup

This thick, sustaining, spicy soup is topped with a fillet of grilled white fish, some natural yogurt and a sprinkling of coriander, making it a nutritious supper dish fit for guests as well as family.

SERVES 4   **PREPARATION** 15 minutes   **COOKING** 30 minutes

1 tbsp sunflower oil

1 large onion, sliced

4 cardamom pods, split

1 tbsp cumin seeds

1 tbsp ground coriander

2 tsp garam masala

2.5cm/1in piece fresh root ginger, peeled and grated

2 red chillies, deseeded and finely sliced

4 large garlic cloves, crushed

2 bay leaves

500g/1lb 2oz butternut squash flesh, cubed

1.25 litres/44fl oz/5 cups vegetable stock

140g/5oz drained and rinsed tinned chickpeas/garbanzo beans

1 tbsp fresh lemon juice

4 thick pollock fillets, about 200g/7oz each

4 tbsp 0% fat Greek yogurt

2 tbsp chopped fresh coriander/cilantro

salt and freshly ground black pepper

1 Heat the oil in a large saucepan and sauté the onion for 7 minutes until softened. Add the spices, garlic and bay leaves and cook for 1 minute. Add the squash, stock and half the chickpeas/garbanzo beans and bring to the boil, then reduce the heat and simmer, half-covered, for 15 minutes until the squash is tender. Remove the bay leaves and cardamom and purée using a stick blender until smooth.

2 Season the soup to taste, add the lemon juice and remaining chickpeas/garbanzo beans, then cook for a further 5 minutes.

3 Meanwhile, preheat the grill to high and line the grill pan with foil. Season the fish, then grill for 3–5 minutes on each side, depending on the thickness of the fillets, until cooked through.

4 Ladle the soup into four large, shallow bowls and top each serving with a fish fillet. Put a spoonful of yogurt on top of the fish and scatter with the coriander/cilantro before serving.

Storage
The soup can be stored in an airtight container in the refrigerator for up to 3 days, then reheated. Cook the fish just before serving.

Health Benefits
Butternut squash is rich in carotenoids – an antioxidant that studies have found to reduce the risk of lung cancer.

Food Facts per Portion
Calories 286kcal • Total Fat 5.4g • saturated fat 0.6g

Oriental Fish en Papillote

These ginger-flavoured fish fillets look good served in their individual parcels, but take care when opening them as the food will be hot and steamy inside. The foil helps to keep the fish moist and succulent during cooking and so very little oil is needed, though a splash of sesame oil adds an oriental flavour. Serve with egg noodles.

SERVES 4   **PREPARATION** 10 minutes   **COOKING** 15 minutes

4 thick white fish fillets, about 175g/6oz each

2 garlic cloves, thinly sliced

6 thin slices fresh root ginger, peeled and cut into thin matchsticks

4 baby leeks, cut into thin strips

1 large carrot, cut into thin strips

1 red bell pepper, deseeded and cut into thin strips

juice of 1 lime

2 tbsp light soy sauce

2 tbsp fresh apple juice

1 tsp sesame oil

salt and freshly ground black pepper

1 Preheat the oven to 200°C/400°F/Gas 6. Put each fillet of fish onto a piece of foil or baking parchment large enough to encase the fish.

2 Divide the garlic, ginger, leeks, carrot and red bell pepper between the fish, placing them on top of the fillets.

3 Mix together the lime juice, soy sauce, apple juice and sesame oil and spoon the mixture over the fish. Season to taste and fold the foil or paper to make 4 loose parcels.

4 Put the parcels on a baking sheet and bake in the preheated oven for 15 minutes until the fish is cooked and opaque. Remove from the oven and serve.

Health Benefits

Leeks contain the same active constituents as other members of the allium family, including onions and garlic. One of these is quercetin, a potent antioxidant that has been found to inhibit carcinogenic development and also restrict the spread of cancer. Vitamins B, C and E are also found in significant amounts.

Food Facts per Portion

Calories 174kcal • Total Fat 2.3g • saturated fat 0.4g

Baked Fish with Spiced Crumb Topping

The orange- and spice-infused crunchy crumb topping gives a pleasant contrast in texture to the succulent fish and crisp vegetables. Serve with new potatoes in their skins.

SERVES 4   **PREPARATION** 15 minutes   **COOKING** 25 minutes

2 slices day-old wholemeal bread, crusts removed and torn into pieces

3 tbsp snipped fresh chives

4 tsp harissa paste

juice and finely grated zest of 1 orange

4 thick white fish fillets, about 175g/6oz each

2 tsp olive oil

350g/12oz fennel, thickly sliced

6 baby leeks, halved lengthways

2 courgettes/zucchinis, halved and sliced lengthways

salt and freshly ground black pepper

1 Preheat the oven to 200°C/400°F/Gas 6. Put the bread in a food processor and pulse to make breadcrumbs. Mix the breadcrumbs with the chives, harissa paste, orange zest and 2 teaspoons of the orange juice, and season well. Spoon the mixture over the fish.

2 Put the oil, fennel, leeks, courgettes/zucchinis and remaining orange juice in a roasting dish; season. Turn the vegetables until they are coated in the oil and juice, then roast in the preheated oven for 10 minutes.

3 Remove the dish from the oven and turn the vegetables again, then put the fish on top. Cook for another 15 minutes or until the fish is cooked and opaque. Remove from the oven and serve.

Health Benefits

Fennel is a well-known diuretic and also has a calming, toning effect on the stomach. It is low in calories and provides excellent amounts of vitamin C, folate, potassium and fibre.

Food Facts per Portion

Calories 218kcal • Total Fat 3.6g • saturated fat 0.5g

Smoked Trout Salad with Dill Dressing

○ ⊘ ☺

Trout is generally an economical fish, and smoked trout is readily available in supermarkets and fishmongers both hot-smoked and cold-smoked. This salad is Scandinavian in inspiration and combines smoked cooked trout, beetroot, dill and a creamy dressing. The perfect accompaniment is the traditional rye bread.

SERVES 4   **PREPARATION** 15 minutes

200g/7oz spinach, rocket and watercress salad

1 small cucumber, coarsely grated

2 shallots, diced

3 cooked beetroot in natural juice, diced

400g/14oz tinned flageolet beans, drained and rinsed

4 hot-smoked, skinless pink trout fillets, about 100g/3½oz each

8 slices rye bread, to serve

Dressing:

2 tbsp light mayonnaise

4 tsp lemon juice

3 tbsp 0% fat Greek yogurt

3 tbsp chopped fresh dill

salt and freshly ground black pepper

1 Mix together the ingredients for the dressing with 1 tablespoon warm water and season to taste.

2 Divide the salad leaves between four plates and arrange the cucumber, shallots, beetroot and beans on top.

3 Place the trout fillets on the salads and spoon over the dressing. Serve with the rye bread on the side.

Health Benefits

Trout is slightly lower in omega-3 fatty acids than salmon but still provides sufficient quantities to be beneficial for the heart, skin and brain function. These fatty acids are not produced in the body and so have to be supplied by diet.

Food Facts per Portion

Calories 375kcal • Total Fat 9.2g • saturated fat 1.7g

Grilled Sole with Herb Sauce

O

Low in fat and simple to prepare, this light and summery fish dish is delicious served with a warm purée of garlicky white beans or mashed potato and steamed long-stem broccoli.

SERVES 4   **PREPARATION** 15 minutes   **COOKING** 6–7 minutes

4 sole or plaice fillets, about 175g/6oz each

2 tsp olive oil

$^{1}/_{2}$ tsp lemon juice

salt and freshly ground black pepper

Herb sauce:

50g/2oz watercress leaves, stems trimmed

large handful rocket

handful fresh basil

handful fresh flat-leaf parsley

4 tbsp light mayonnaise

2 tbsp lemon juice

1   Preheat the grill to high and line the grill pan with foil.

2   Steam the watercress and rocket for 1$^{1}/_{2}$ minutes until wilted. Rinse the leaves under cold running water and drain well. Gently squeeze out any water left in the leaves with your hands.

3 Put the watercress and rocket in a food processor or blender with the remaining ingredients for the herb sauce and blend to a sauce consistency.

4 Lightly brush the sole with the oil and season. Cook the sole under the preheated grill for 4–5 minutes, squeeze over the lemon juice and serve with a spoonful of the herb sauce.

Storage

The herb sauce can be stored in an airtight container in the refrigerator for up to 3 days.

Health Benefits

Peppery-flavoured watercress is a member of the cruciferous group of vegetables, which are highly valued for their cancer-prohibiting properties. It is an excellent source of vitamins B1, B2, B6, C and E along with iron, calcium, copper and potassium.

Food Facts per Portion

Calories 201kcal • Total Fat 8.4g • saturated fat 1.2g

Sole with Orange Dressing

Fish is the perfect low-fat food and very quick to cook. Serve this dish with mangetout and broccoli and some wholemeal bread.

SERVES 4   **PREPARATION** 10 minutes   **COOKING** 5 minutes

4 sole or plaice fillets, about 175g/6oz each

1 tsp lemon juice

salt and freshly ground black pepper

Orange dressing:

4 tbsp fresh orange juice

1 tsp lemon juice

2 tsp extra-virgin olive oil

3 tbsp finely chopped fresh flat-leaf parsley

1 shallot, diced

1 Preheat the grill to high and line the pan with foil. Season the fish and grill for 5 minutes until cooked. Squeeze lemon juice over.

2 Mix the dressing ingredients together and season well. Spoon the dressing over the fish before serving.

Health Benefits

Parsley is packed with vitamin C and beta carotene.

Food Facts per Portion

Calories 159kcal • Total Fat 4g • saturated fat 0.6g

Halibut Tricolore

The pesto sauce and melted mozzarella make a rich topping for the halibut steaks. Serve with new potatoes and a green salad.

SERVES 4   **PREPARATION** 15 minutes   **COOKING** 8 minutes

1 tbsp lemon juice

4 halibut steaks, about 175g/6oz each

2 tbsp light pesto

2 vine-ripened tomatoes, sliced

150g/5½oz ball light mozzarella cheese, drained and cut into 8 slices

salt and freshly ground black pepper

1   Preheat the grill to high and line a grill pan with foil. Brush the lemon juice over the halibut. Grill the fish for 3 minutes, then turn over and cook for a further 2 minutes or until almost cooked and opaque.

2   Top each halibut steak with some of the pesto, followed by a few slices of tomato and then 2 slices of the mozzarella. Grill for another 2–3 minutes until the mozzarella has melted and is slightly golden. Season to taste, then serve.

Health Benefits

The red pigment lycopene in tomatoes has been found to lower the risk of certain cancers, including prostate and lung.

Food Facts per Portion

Calories 337kcal • Total Fat 14.4g • saturated fat 5.3g

Halibut with Tomato & Red Onion Relish

Halibut is a firm, white, nutrient-dense fish with a delicate, slightly sweet flavour that is complemented here by the zingy relish. This delicious fish supper contains minimal amounts of oil but is nevertheless full of flavour. Serve with couscous and steamed green beans.

SERVES 4   PREPARATION 10 minutes   COOKING 6–8 minutes

4 halibut steaks, about 175g/6oz each

2 tsp lime juice

salt and freshly ground black pepper

Red onion relish:

8 vine-ripened tomatoes, deseeded and diced

1 small red onion, finely diced

1 garlic clove, crushed

2 tbsp lime juice

1 long red chilli, roughly chopped

4 tbsp chopped fresh flat-leaf parsley

1 Preheat the grill to high and line the grill pan with foil. Put the halibut on the grill pan, brush with the lime juice and season. Grill for 3–4 minutes on each side or until cooked and opaque.

2 Meanwhile, mix all the red onion relish ingredients together in a bowl. Season with salt and turn gently until all the ingredients are combined.

3 Serve the halibut with the relish spooned over the top.

Storage

The red onion relish can be stored in an airtight container in the refrigerator for up to 2 days.

Health Benefits

A recent study showed that eating fish on a regular basis reduces the risk of certain types of strokes. It revealed that women who ate fish 2 to 4 times per week had a 27 per cent reduced risk of a stroke compared to women who ate fish just once a month.

Food Facts per Portion

Calories 211kcal • Total Fat 3.8g • saturated fat 0.7g

Salmon in Black Bean Sauce

This quick Chinese-style dish makes a great weekday supper.
All you need to add is some steamed green vegetables to make
a complete meal. Hoisin sauce or teriyaki sauce can be used
instead of the black bean sauce. If preferred, the salmon can be
served with brown basmati rice.

SERVES 4   **PREPARATION** 10 minutes   **COOKING** 10–12 minutes

4 salmon fillets, about 140g/5oz each

2 tsp lemon juice

250g/9oz wholemeal noodles

2 tsp sunflower oil

2 garlic cloves, crushed

6 tbsp black bean sauce

2.5cm/1in piece fresh root ginger, peeled and grated

6 tbsp fresh orange juice

salt and freshly ground black pepper

1   Preheat the grill to high and line the grill pan with foil. Arrange
    the salmon fillets in the grill pan, squeeze over the lemon
    juice and cook for about 10–12 minutes, or until cooked,
    turning halfway.

2   While the salmon is grilling, cook the noodles following the
    packet instructions, then drain.

3 Meanwhile, heat the oil and fry the garlic for 30 seconds, stirring continuously, until softened. Stir in the black bean sauce, ginger and orange juice, then heat through until slightly reduced and thickened.

4 Place the salmon on four plates and spoon the sauce over the top; season to taste. Serve with the noodles.

Health Benefits

Much prized and celebrated, garlic has been praised for its numerous medicinal properties for centuries. Cooking does not inhibit garlic's anti-cancer, blood-thinning and decongestant capabilities. This superfood has also been found to reduce blood cholesterol and high blood pressure.

Food Facts per Portion

Calories 539kcal • Total Fat 21.3g • saturated fat 2.8g

Tilapia with Coriander/ Cilantro Houmous

O

Reduced-fat humous is now readily available in shops and makes a great base for a sauce or dressing flavoured with lime and coriander. Serve this dish with couscous and a green salad.

SERVES 4	**PREPARATION** 10 minutes	**COOKING** 6 minutes

4 tilapia fillets, about 175g/6oz each

2 tsp olive oil

2 tbsp lime juice

1 tsp paprika

salt and freshly ground black pepper

Coriander/cilantro humous:

4 tbsp reduced-fat humous

2 tbsp chopped fresh coriander/cilantro, plus extra for sprinkling

1 tsp finely grated lime zest

1 tbsp light mayonnaise

1 Preheat the grill to high and line the grill pan with foil. Brush the tilapia fillets with the oil and drizzle over half of the lime juice; season well.

2 Sprinkle the fillets with the paprika and cook under the preheated grill for 4–6 minutes, turning halfway, until the fish is cooked.

3   Meanwhile, mix together the houmous, coriander/cilantro, lime
     zest, reserved lime juice and mayonnaise, then season to taste.
     Place the tilapia on plates, scatter with the extra coriander/
     cilantro and serve with the flavoured humous.

Storage

The flavoured humous can be stored in an airtight container in the
refrigerator for up to 3 days.

Health Benefits

The lime, like other citrus fruit, is known for its generous vitamin C
content, which boosts the body's ability to absorb iron from food
and can also alleviate the severity and length of colds and flu.
Vitamin C is destroyed by heat and is therefore more readily
available in uncooked food.

Food Facts per Portion

Calories 201kcal • Total Fat 6.1g • saturated fat 0.9g

Sea Bass with Japanese-style Pickled Vegetables

Fresh and rejuvenating, this simple fish dish has all the lightness of classic Japanese dishes. Serve the sea bass with rice noodles and steamed asparagus.

SERVES 4

PREPARATION 15 minutes, plus marinating   **COOKING** 4 minutes

4 sea bass fillets, about 175g/6oz each

3 tbsp lime juice

2 tsp balsamic vinegar

1 garlic clove, crushed

2 red chillies, deseeded and finely chopped

torn fresh basil, to scatter

salt

Pickled vegetables:

2 carrots, finely shredded

1 small cucumber, deseeded and finely shredded

4 spring onions/scallions, finely shredded

4 tbsp rice vinegar

1 Put the sea bass, skin-side down, in a shallow dish. Mix together the lime juice, balsamic vinegar, garlic and chillies. Pour the mixture over the fish and season with salt, then cover and leave to marinate in the refrigerator for 30 minutes. Occasionally, spoon the marinade over the fillets.

2 To make the pickled vegetables, put the carrot, cucumber and spring onions/scallions in a bowl. Pour over the vinegar, season, and turn until combined. Set aside.

3 Preheat the grill to high and line the grill pan with foil. Put the sea bass, skin-side up, on the grill pan and brush with the marinade. Grill for 3–4 minutes until the skin becomes crisp and the fish is cooked and opaque.

4 Drain the pickled vegetables. Place the sea bass and the vegetables on four plates, scatter with basil and serve.

Health Benefits

Carrots are one of the richest sources of carotenoids, found in orange, yellow and red vegetables. Carotenoids are antioxidants that slow down or prevent cell damage from free radical oxidation in the body. Studies have found that a single carrot a day could reduce the rate of lung cancer by half.

Food Facts per Portion

Calories 191kcal • Total Fat 4.5g • saturated fat 0.7g

Steamed Trout Parcels

Light and fragrant, these stuffed fish parcels just need the addition of soba (buckwheat) noodles and pak choi/bok choy to make a complete meal.

SERVES 4   **PREPARATION** 20 minutes   **COOKING** 15 minutes

1 tbsp sunflower oil

5 spring onions/scallions, finely chopped

5cm/2in piece fresh root ginger, peeled and grated

5cm/2in piece lemongrass stalk, tough outer leaves removed and inside finely chopped

4 tbsp chopped fresh coriander/cilantro

juice and finely grated zest of 2 limes

8 skinned pink trout fillets, about 70g/2$\frac{1}{2}$oz each

6 large lettuce leaves

salt and freshly ground black pepper

lemon wedges, to serve

1 Heat the oil in a wok and stir-fry the spring onions/scallions, ginger and lemongrass for 1 minute. Remove from the heat and mix with the coriander/cilantro and the lime juice and zest.

2 Lay the fish fillets on a plate and season. Arrange the spring onion/scallion mixture down the centre of each fillet, then carefully roll the fillet up from the thinnest end. Secure each parcel with 1 or 2 cocktail sticks.

3 Put 2 of the lettuce leaves in the bottom of a steamer and top with 4 of the fish parcels, then steam for about 6 minutes until cooked and opaque. Remove the parcels from the steamer and keep warm, covered, while you cook the remaining fish rolls.

4 Arrange the rest of the lettuce leaves on four plates and top each one with 2 fillets. Serve with lemon wedges.

Health Benefits

Trout is part of the oily fish family, and while it certainly contains more fat than white fish, it is the beneficial omega-3 type, so it's well worth trying to eat the recommended 1–2 servings per week. Omega-3 fatty acids help to relax the walls of blood vessels, which reduces the risk of blood clotting and aids circulation.

Food Facts per Portion

Calories 188kcal • Total Fat 8.2g • saturated fat 0.4g

Hoki with Chilli-orange Glaze

Hoki is classified as a sustainable white fish and makes a suitable alternative to cod, haddock and other endangered species. It has a delicate flavour and succulent texture and is low in fat. Serve this dish with brown rice and steamed green vegetables.

SERVES 4　　　**PREPARATION** 15 minutes　　　**COOKING** 10–12 minutes

4 thick hoki fillets, about 175g/6oz each

2 tsp olive oil

juice and finely grated zest of 1 orange

2 tbsp sweet chilli sauce

2 tbsp chopped fresh coriander/cilantro

salt and freshly ground black pepper

1 Preheat the grill to high and line the grill pan with foil. Brush the hoki with the oil, and season. Grill the fish for 5 minutes.

2 Meanwhile, mix together the orange juice and zest and sweet chilli sauce. Season well.

3 Remove the fish from the grill and turn over. Spoon half of the orange sauce over the fish and grill for another 3–5 minutes until the fish is cooked and the sauce has formed a sticky glaze.

4 Put the remaining sauce in a saucepan and heat through gently until thickened. Serve the fish with the sauce spooned over and scattered with coriander/cilantro.

Health Benefits

The dense white flesh of hoki is rich in omega-3 fatty acids. There is widespread concern that diets do not contain a sufficient quantity of this type of fat, which has been shown to improve mood and alleviate feelings of depression.

Food Facts per Portion

Calories 175kcal • Total Fat 4.9g • saturated fat 0.7g

Variation

The chilli-orange glaze also works well with oily types of fish, such as salmon, trout and mackerel.

Moules Marinière

Mussels are one of the most environmentally sound types of seafood. They're also inexpensive to buy, quick to prepare and available in abundance. Serve with a wholemeal seeded baguette for dunking into the juices, and a mixed leaf salad by the side.

SERVES 4 **PREPARATION** 25 minutes **COOKING** 12–14 minutes

1.5kg/3lb 5oz mussels

1 tbsp olive oil

1 large onion, finely chopped

4 garlic cloves, finely chopped

250ml/9fl oz/1 cup dry white wine

2 tbsp half-fat crème fraiche

4 tbsp chopped fresh flat-leaf parsley

1 Rinse the mussels in a sink of cold water and discard any that stay open when tapped. Scrape off any barnacles and pull away the beards, then rinse again a couple of times to get rid of any sand.

2 Heat the oil in a large, deep saucepan with a lid. Add the onion and sauté, covered, for 6 minutes, stirring frequently, until softened. Add the garlic and sauté for 1 minute more.

3 Add the mussels, then pour in the wine and stir. Cover and cook over a high heat, shaking the pan occasionally, for 3–5 minutes or until the mussels have opened. Discard any that remain shut.

4   Scoop out the mussels using a slotted spoon and divide
    between four warm, large bowls.

5   Stir the crème fraîche into the cooking liquid and warm
    through for 1 minute, then pour the sauce over the mussels
    before sprinkling with parsley and serving.

Health Benefits

A good source of omega-3 fatty acids, mussels also provide
selenium, zinc, iodine and copper. The mineral zinc is crucial for
memory and concentration. Studies have shown that even a mild
deficiency can impair mental function, leading to irritability and
mood swings.

Food Facts per Portion

Calories 358kcal • Total Fat 10.2g • saturated fat 2.6g

Provençal Prawns/Shrimp

Convenience food doesn't have to be junk food. Cooked prawns/shrimp are a perfect example, as they can be served as they are or briefly heated before being eaten. Serve with a crusty baguette and a rocket salad.

SERVES 4   **PREPARATION** 10 minutes   **COOKING** 12 minutes

1 tbsp olive oil

3 garlic cloves, chopped

420ml/14$\frac{1}{2}$fl oz/1$\frac{2}{3}$ cups sugocasa or passata

1 tbsp sun-dried tomato paste

$\frac{1}{2}$ tsp smoked paprika

4 tbsp small pitted black olives, rinsed

400g/14oz tinned butter beans in water, drained and rinsed

400g/14oz cooked and peeled large prawns/shrimp

fresh oregano, to scatter

salt and freshly ground black pepper

1 Heat the oil in a frying pan and fry the garlic for 30 seconds, stirring continuously to prevent it burning.

2 Add the sugocasa, tomato paste, smoked paprika, olives and butter beans and cook, stirring occasionally, over a medium-low heat for 10 minutes until reduced and thickened.

3 Add the prawns/shrimp and heat through for 1 minute, then season to taste and scatter with oregano before serving.

Storage

The tomato sauce can be stored in an airtight container in the refrigerator for up to 5 days or in a freezer for up to 3 months. Reheat and add the prawns/shrimp.

Health Benefits

Seafood, such as prawns/shrimp, is a source of the amino acid tyrosine, which has been linked to increased mental function and alertness. Prawns/shrimp are also a good source of zinc.

Food Facts per Portion

Calories 214kcal • Total Fat 5.3g • saturated fat 0.9g

Poached Eggs with Spiced Chickpeas

V **O**

Poaching is an ideal method of cooking, whether for vegetables, eggs, fish or poultry. Not only is it quick but it also does not require any fat for successful results. This warm salad makes a quick and filling meal served with new potatoes.

SERVES 4	PREPARATION 15 minutes	COOKING 7 minutes

1 tbsp olive oil

2 large garlic cloves, finely chopped

2 tsp cumin seeds

400g/14oz tinned chickpeas/garbanzo beans in water, drained and rinsed

400g/14oz/4$\frac{1}{2}$ cups baby spinach leaves

4 tbsp lemon juice

$\frac{1}{2}$ tsp crushed dried chillies

4 eggs

salt and freshly ground black pepper

1 Heat the oil in a large non-stick frying pan and fry the garlic and cumin for 30 seconds until softened. Add the chickpeas/ garbanzo beans, spinach, lemon juice, crushed dried chillies and 2 tablespoons water and cook for 3 minutes, turning occasionally, or until the spinach has wilted and everything is heated through; season generously to taste. Remove from the heat and put a lid on to keep warm.

2 Bring a sauté pan of water to the boil, then reduce the heat to a simmer. Break one of the eggs into a cup, gently swirl the water with a spoon, then slip the egg into the water; repeat with the other 3 eggs so that all enter the water quite soon after each other. (The moving water helps the eggs to keep their shape.) Cook at a gentle simmer for 2–3 minutes until the white of each egg is firm but the yolk is still runny (i.e. has not turned pale).

3 Spoon the chickpea/garbanzo bean mixture onto four plates. Lift out the eggs with a slotted spoon, drain, and place on top of the chickpeas/garbanzo beans, then serve.

Health Benefits

Spinach is a rich source of iron, but it is advisable to combine it with a vitamin C-rich food to aid its absorption by the body. Spinach is also a good source of vitamin B6, calcium, folate, thiamine and zinc.

Food Facts per Portion

Calories 207kcal • Total Fat 10.9g • saturated fat 2.2g

Bean, Fennel & Red Bell Pepper Salad

This simple supper for four makes use of tinned beans, which are excellent for adding nutritional value, protein and substance to a meal. Serve with some new potatoes or couscous.

SERVES 4	PREPARATION 10 minutes	COOKING 5 minutes

1 tbsp olive oil

1 large red bell pepper, deseeded and sliced into strips

1 large fennel bulb, sliced

2 garlic cloves, finely chopped

4 tbsp fresh oregano

4 tsp balsamic vinegar

400g/14oz tinned flageolet beans in water, drained and rinsed

4 large tortillas

4 tbsp reduced-fat humous

1 red chilli, deseeded and chopped

salt and freshly ground black pepper

1 Heat the oil in a large non-stick frying pan and sauté the red bell pepper, fennel and garlic for 2–3 minutes until softened; add 1–2 tablespoons water to the pan if it becomes too dry.

2   Remove from the heat and stir in the oregano, balsamic
    vinegar and beans. Season well and stir until everything is
    combined, then serve. Alternatively, leave until cold.

3   Just before serving, warm the tortillas, 2 at a time, in a dry
    frying pan. Spoon the bean salad on top, followed by the
    humous, and scatter the chilli over the mixture.

Storage

The salad can be stored in an airtight container in the refrigerator
for up to 2 days, then served cold.

Health Benefits

Beans contain both the soluble and insoluble type of fibre. Soluble
fibre has been found to reduce cholesterol levels, reducing the risk
of heart disease and strokes, while insoluble fibre ensures regular
bowel movements.

Food Facts per Portion

Calories 180kcal • Total Fat 3.9g • saturated fat 0.5g

Oriental Omelette Parcel

Ⓥ Ⓞ ◍ ◍

An omelette makes the perfect wrap for these lightly steamed vegetables in black bean sauce. Serve on a bed of egg noodles.

SERVES 2   **PREPARATION** 15 minutes   **COOKING** 5–7 minutes

115g/4oz long-stem broccoli, stalks trimmed

1 carrot, cut into thin sticks

2 spring onions/scallions, cut into strips

1cm/ ½in piece fresh root ginger, peeled and finely grated

1 red chilli, deseeded and thinly sliced

handful beansprouts

2 tbsp chopped fresh coriander/cilantro

2 tbsp black bean sauce

1 tsp soy sauce

2 large/extra large eggs, lightly beaten

1 tbsp sunflower oil

salt and freshly ground black pepper

1 Steam the broccoli and carrot for 4–5 minutes or until just tender. Refresh under cold running water, then put in a saucepan with the spring onions/scallions, ginger, chilli, beansprouts, coriander/cilantro, black bean sauce and soy sauce. Season to taste and stir until combined.

2 While the vegetables are steaming, lightly beat one of the eggs in a bowl, then season. Pour half of the oil into a non-stick frying pan and wipe with a piece of crumpled kitchen towel until there is a light coating of oil over the base of the pan. Heat the pan until hot.

3 Pour the beaten egg into the pan and swirl until it covers the base in a thin layer. Cook the egg until set, then turn out onto a plate and keep warm while you make a second omelette, adding the remaining oil first, if necessary.

4 Just before serving, warm the black bean vegetables over a low heat for 1–2 minutes, stirring occasionally. To serve, spoon half of the vegetables down the middle of each omelette and roll up loosely. Cut diagonally in half crossways so the filling is visible.

Health Benefits

Broccoli is packed with nutrients, including phytochemicals – plant compounds that studies have shown to play a crucial role in fighting disease by stimulating the body's defences. Eating cruciferous vegetables, such as broccoli, at least 4 times a week may reduce the risk of cancer of the lung, breast, colon, ovary, uterus and prostate.

Food Facts per Portion

Calories 172kcal • Total Fat 11.7g • saturated fat 2.3g

Spring Vegetable Stir-fry with Cashew Nuts

The secret to a successful stir-fry is preparation: it's a good idea to have all the ingredients to hand before you start, and the vegetables cut and liquids measured. Stir-fries require the minimum of oil and because the vegetables are cooked briefly they retain most of their precious vitamins and minerals. Serve with brown rice.

SERVES 4   **PREPARATION** 10 minutes   **COOKING** 5–7 minutes

1 tbsp sunflower oil

350g/12oz broccoli, cut into small florets

1 large onion, sliced on the diagonal

175g/6oz asparagus spears, trimmed

4 heads pak choi/bok choy, sliced lengthways in half

2 large garlic cloves, chopped

2.5cm/1in piece fresh root ginger, peeled and finely chopped

3 spring onions/scallions, sliced on the diagonal

5 tbsp fresh orange juice

2 tbsp soy sauce

1 tsp toasted sesame oil

55g/2oz/½ cup unsalted cashew nuts, toasted and chopped

torn fresh basil, to scatter

1 Heat a wok until hot then pour in the sunflower oil. Add the
   broccoli, onion and asparagus. Stir-fry the vegetables for
   3–4 minutes, adding a splash of water if the wok appears dry.

2 Add the pak choi/bok choy, garlic, ginger and spring onions/
   scallions and stir-fry for 1 more minute.

3 Pour in the orange juice, soy sauce and sesame oil and stir-fry
   for a further 1–2 minutes until the vegetables have softened
   but still retain some bite.

4 Scatter the cashew nuts over the stir-fry and scatter with the
   basil before serving.

Health Benefits

The value of vegetables cannot be underestimated. In the USA,
the National Institute for Health recommends eating 4–5 servings
of vegetables a day, whereas in the UK the advice is to eat just
5 servings of vegetables and fruits combined. By eating lots of
vegetables, you can significantly reduce blood pressure and cholesterol levels and help to reduce the risk of diabetes.

Food Facts per Portion

Calories 208kcal • Total Fat 12.8g • saturated fat 2.1g

Herby Ricotta Flan

V O ⊜

This light, summery flan is so delicious it does not need a
high-fat pastry case, and the roasted tomatoes are the perfect
accompaniment. Serve with roasted new potatoes.

SERVES 8 **PREPARATION** 20 minutes **COOKING** 1 hour

---

1 tsp olive oil

750g/1lb 10 oz/3 cups ricotta cheese

70g/2¹/₂oz/scant 1 cup Parmesan cheese, finely grated

3 eggs, separated

¹/₂ tsp salt

4 tbsp torn fresh basil, plus whole leaves to scatter

4 tbsp fresh oregano, plus extra to scatter

¹/₂ tsp paprika, to dust

Roasted tomatoes:

400g/14oz vine-ripened cherry tomatoes

1 tbsp balsamic vinegar

freshly ground black pepper

1 Preheat the oven to 180°C/350°F/Gas 4 and lightly grease a
20cm/8in springform cake tin with a little of the olive oil. Put
the ricotta, Parmesan, egg yolks and salt in a food processor
and blend until smooth and creamy. Turn the mixture out into
a bowl and stir in the basil and oregano.

2 Whisk the egg whites in a grease-free bowl until they form stiff peaks. Using a metal spoon, gently fold the egg whites into the ricotta mixture.

3 Spoon the mixture into the prepared tin and smooth with a palette knife. Bake in the preheated oven for about 45 minutes.

4 Just before the 45 minutes are up, put the tomatoes in a roasting tin, pour over the remaining oil and the balsamic vinegar and season, then turn the tomatoes in the mixture. Add the tomatoes to the oven and cook for 15 minutes (making a total of 1 hour for the tart) until the tart has risen and the top is light golden and the tomatoes have softened and caramelized slightly.

5 Remove the tart and the tomatoes from the oven. Leave the tart to cool slightly before removing from the tin. Dust with the paprika and serve cut into wedges with the roasted tomatoes, scattered with the basil and oregano.

Storage
The flan and roasted tomatoes can be stored in an airtight container in the refrigerator for up to 3 days.

Health Benefits
Ricotta is rich in protein and a good source of calcium and magnesium, which work together to reduce high blood pressure.

Food Facts per Portion
Calories 214kcal • Total Fat 15.6g • saturated fat 8.9g

Mushroom & Spinach Open Lasagne

🅥 🅕 🅖 🅐 🅞

A classic lasagne is usually high in fat, but this vegetarian version is much lower in fat as well as quick and simple to make.

SERVES 4   **PREPARATION** 15 minutes   **COOKING** 25 minutes

85g/3oz dried porcini mushrooms

2 tbsp olive oil

200g/7oz field mushrooms, sliced

3 large garlic cloves, chopped

2 tsp dried oregano

200ml/7fl oz/generous ³/₄ cup dry white wine

200g/7oz/generous ³/₄ cup tinned chopped tomatoes

200g/7oz/2 cups spinach, tough stalks removed, rinsed well and shredded

8 fresh lasagne sheets

40g/1¹/₂oz/¹/₂ cup Parmesan shavings

handful torn fresh basil, to scatter

salt and freshly ground black pepper

1 Put the porcini mushrooms in a small bowl and cover with hot water. Leave to soak for 15 minutes, then drain, rinse and pat dry.

2 Heat the oil in a large sauté pan, add the porcini and sauté over a medium-high heat for 5 minutes until they become

slightly crisp around the edges. Add the field mushrooms, garlic and oregano and cook for a further 5 minutes, stirring regularly.

3 Pour in the wine and bring to the boil, then reduce the heat and simmer for 3 minutes until reduced. Stir in the tomatoes and spinach and cook for a further 10 minutes, half-covered, stirring occasionally, until reduced and thickened; season to taste.

4 Meanwhile, cook the lasagne sheets in plenty of boiling water for about 3 minutes. Drain lightly – the pasta should still be moist.

5 Place a sheet of lasagne on each plate, divide the mushroom and spinach sauce between them, then top with a second sheet. Season and scatter with the Parmesan and basil before serving.

Storage

The mushroom and spinach sauce can be prepared up to 2 days in advance and stored in an airtight container in the refrigerator. Reheat before completing the recipe.

Health Benefits

Mushrooms are a useful source of vitamins B1, B2 and niacin, which work in tandem and are essential for energy production, growth and mental function. They are also a good source of the minerals potassium and iron.

Food Facts per Portion

Calories 207kcal • Total Fat 11.1g • saturated fat 3.6g

Mixed Bean & Vegetable Tagine

This Moroccan-inspired dish makes use of tinned beans for convenience and to save time, but you could cook your own dried beans instead. If you don't want to use mixed beans, chickpeas/garbanzo beans are a good alternative. Serve with couscous.

SERVES 4   **PREPARATION** 15 minutes   **COOKING** 35 minutes

1 tbsp olive oil

1 large onion, roughly chopped

3 large garlic cloves, chopped

1 small butternut squash, peeled, deseeded and cut into
    2cm/³/₄in chunks

2 courgettes/zucchinis, sliced

1 tbsp cumin seeds

1 tbsp ras-el-hanout

1 tsp chilli powder

400g/14oz/1²/₃ cups tinned chopped tomatoes

250ml/9fl oz/1 cup vegetable stock

1 tbsp honey

2 tbsp tomato paste

400g/14oz tinned mixed beans in water, drained and rinsed

handful fresh coriander/cilantro

salt and freshly ground black pepper

1   Heat the oil in a large, heavy-based saucepan and sauté the
    onion for 7 minutes until softened, then add the garlic, squash
    and courgettes/zucchinis and cook, stirring occasionally, over
    a medium-low heat for 5 minutes. Add the spices and cook for
    a further minute, stirring continuously.

2   Pour in the tomatoes, stock, honey and tomato paste. Bring
    to the boil, then reduce the heat and simmer, half-covered,
    for 10 minutes until the sauce begins to thicken.

3   Add the mixed beans and half of the coriander/cilantro and
    cook, half-covered, for a further 10 minutes, stirring occasionally
    (adding extra stock if the sauce appears too thick). Season and
    scatter with the remaining coriander/cilantro before serving.

Storage

The tagine can be stored in an airtight container in the refrigerator
for up to 3 days or the freezer for up to 3 months, then reheated.

Health Benefits

Courgettes/zucchinis or summer squash are effective diuretics and,
because of their high water content, are low in calories. Their
potassium content means that they benefit people who suffer from
high blood pressure.

Food Facts per Portion

Calories 161kcal • Total Fat 3.4g • saturated fat 0.4g

Vegetable Goulash

This warming stew contains an abundance of healthy vegetables and makes a great supper dish served on a winter's day with brown rice or rye bread.

SERVES 4   **PREPARATION** 15 minutes   **COOKING** 35 minutes

1 tbsp olive oil

1 large onion, roughly chopped

2 large garlic cloves, chopped

1 large red bell pepper, deseeded and diced

300g/10$\frac{1}{2}$oz butternut squash flesh, diced

150g/5$\frac{1}{2}$oz chestnut mushrooms, halved

2 tsp caraway seeds

1 tbsp paprika

2 tsp plain flour

400g/14oz/1$\frac{2}{3}$ cups tinned chopped tomatoes

400g/14oz tinned cannellini beans, drained and rinsed

250ml/9fl oz/1 cup vegetable stock

4 tsp half-fat sour cream

salt and freshly ground black pepper

1   Heat the oil in a large, heavy-based saucepan. Add the onion
    and sauté, half-covered, for 8 minutes until softened. Add the
    garlic, red bell pepper, squash, mushrooms and caraway seeds
    and cook, half-covered, for 8 minutes, stirring occasionally,
    until the vegetables have softened.

2   Stir in the paprika and flour and cook for 1 minute, then add the
    tomatoes, cannellini beans and stock. Bring to the boil, then
    reduce the heat and simmer, half-covered, for about 15 minutes
    until the vegetables are tender and the sauce has thickened.

3   Add the sour cream and warm through, stirring, then season
    before serving.

Storage

Can be stored in an airtight container in the refrigerator for up
to 3 days or the freezer for up to 3 months, then reheated.

Health Benefits

Red bell peppers are rich in antioxidants, including beta carotene,
lycopene and vitamin C, which help to promote mental alertness
and memory by protecting nerve cells in the brain.

Food Facts per Portion

Calories 164kcal • Total Fat 4.1g • saturated fat 0.9g

Creamy Puy Lentils with Poached Eggs

Ⓥ Ⓞ ◉ ◉ ◉

Puy lentils are blue-grey pulses from France. They keep their shape when cooked and are delicious in warm salads, stews or soups.

SERVES 4   **PREPARATION** 15 minutes   **COOKING** 30 minutes

225g/8oz/1 cup Puy lentils, rinsed

1 tbsp olive oil

1 large red bell pepper, deseeded and diced

3 large garlic cloves, chopped

juice and finely grated zest of 1 lemon

2 tsp dried oregano

1 tbsp half-fat crème fraîche

1 tbsp Dijon mustard

6 tbsp vegetable stock

2 tbsp chopped fresh flat-leaf parsley

4 eggs

salt and freshly ground black pepper

1 Put the lentils in a saucepan, cover with water and bring to the boil, then reduce the heat and simmer, covered, for 25 minutes or until tender. Drain.

2 Meanwhile, heat the oil in a frying pan and fry the red bell pepper and garlic for 3 minutes, stirring frequently.

3   Add the cooked lentils, lemon juice and zest, oregano, crème fraîche, mustard, stock and 3 tablespoons water. Season and heat through over a medium heat, then stir in the parsley. Remove from the heat and put a lid on to keep warm.

4   Bring a sauté pan of water to the boil, then reduce the heat to a simmer. Break one of the eggs into a cup, gently swirl the water with a spoon, then slip the egg into the water; repeat with the other 3 eggs so that all enter the water quite soon after each other. (The moving water helps the eggs to keep their shape.) Cook at a gentle simmer for 2–3 minutes until the white of each egg is firm but the yolk is still runny (i.e. has not turned pale). Remove with a slotted spoon and serve on top of the lentils.

Storage

The lentil mixture can be prepared up to 3 days in advance and either served at room temperature or gently reheated.

Health Benefits

Eggs provide the body with choline, which studies have shown to be useful for people with early stages of memory loss. They are also a complete protein, making them a valuable food for vegetarians, since it is one of the few non-meat sources that provide all the essential amino acids necessary to build neurotransmitters – the brain's messengers.

Food Facts per Portion

Calories 293kcal • Total Fat 10.2g • saturated fat 2.5g

Thai Green Vegetable Curry

Homemade green Thai paste produces an aromatic, fresh-tasting curry, and is very easy to make. Serve the curry with brown rice.

SERVES 4   **PREPARATION** 25 minutes   **COOKING** 20 minutes

1 tbsp sunflower oil

250g/9oz block tofu, patted dry with kitchen paper and cubed

200ml/7fl oz/generous ¾ cup half-fat coconut milk

350ml/12fl oz/scant 1½ cups vegetable stock

200g/7oz sweet potato, peeled and cubed

250g/9oz long-stem broccoli, trimmed

8 baby corn, halved lengthways

1 large orange bell pepper, deseeded and sliced

150g/5½oz/1½ cups spinach, tough stalks removed, rinsed well and shredded

salt and freshly ground black pepper

Spice paste:

5 green chillies, deseeded and chopped

2 lemongrass stalks, peeled and inside finely chopped

2 shallots, sliced

juice and finely grated zest of 2 limes

2 garlic cloves, chopped

2 tsp ground coriander

2 tsp ground cumin

2.5cm/1in piece fresh root ginger, peeled and grated

4 tbsp chopped fresh coriander/cilantro, plus extra to scatter

1 Put all the ingredients for the spice paste in a food processor and blend to make a fairly coarse paste.

2 Heat the oil in a large wok or saucepan and stir-fry the tofu for 5 minutes until light golden. Remove, then add the spice paste and cook for 2 minutes, stirring. Pour in the coconut milk, stock and sweet potato and bring to the boil, then reduce the heat and simmer for 10 minutes until reduced.

3 Add the broccoli, baby corn and orange bell pepper and cook for 5 minutes. Next, add the spinach and tofu and cook for another 2 minutes until the vegetables are just tender. Season the curry to taste and scatter with the extra coriander/cilantro before serving.

Storage

The Thai curry paste can be stored in an airtight container in the refrigerator for up to 2 weeks.

Health Benefits

Chillies are a great endorphin booster – the body's feel-good chemicals – and have the ability to improve circulation and act as a decongestant.

Food Facts per Portion

Calories 186kcal • Total Fat 8.1g • saturated fat 1.1g

Lentil & Vegetable Dahl

There is something very sustaining and nourishing about dahl, which makes it a perfect dish when you are looking for something warming and filling. Ideally make it a day in advance, then reheat, to let the spices infuse. Serve with warm wholemeal chapattis.

SERVES 4   **PREPARATION** 20 minutes   **COOKING** 40–45 minutes

1 tbsp sunflower oil

1 large onion, roughly chopped

4 large garlic cloves, chopped

1 large carrot, cut into small dice

5cm/2in piece fresh root ginger, peeled and grated

2 tsp cumin seeds

4 cardamom pods, split

2 bay leaves

2 tsp ground turmeric

1–2 tsp chilli powder

1 tbsp garam masala

225g/8oz/1 cup split red lentils

125ml/4fl oz/$\frac{1}{2}$ cup half-fat coconut milk

5 tbsp tinned chopped tomatoes

juice of 1$\frac{1}{2}$ limes

4 tbsp chopped fresh coriander/cilantro, plus extra to serve

salt and freshly ground black pepper

1 Heat the oil in a large saucepan and sauté the onion for 7 minutes until softened. Add the garlic, carrot, ginger, cumin, cardamom and bay leaves and cook for 3 minutes, stirring continuously, until the carrot begins to soften. Stir in the ground spices.

2 Next, add the lentils, coconut milk, tomatoes and 455ml/16fl oz/ scant 2 cups water. Bring to the boil and stir, then reduce the heat and simmer, covered, for 25–30 minutes or until the lentils are tender (you may need to add a little more water if they appear dry). Stir occasionally to prevent them sticking.

3 Stir in the lime juice and coriander/cilantro. Season to taste and cook for another minute. Serve scattered with the extra coriander/cilantro.

Storage

Can be stored in an airtight container in the refrigerator for up to 3 days or the freezer for up to 3 months, then reheated.

Health Benefits

Extremely low in fat and richer in protein than many other pulses, lentils are also a good source of fibre, which aids the functioning of the bowels and colon. Fibre slows downs the rate at which sugars enters the bloodstream, helping to provide you with a steady supply of energy.

Food Facts per Portion

Calories 232kcal • Total Fat 3.8g • saturated fat 0.5g

Greek Salad

This classic salad is made using a handful of simple ingredients. Serve with warm pitta bread and a spoonful of reduced-fat humous for a light summery supper dish.

SERVES 4   **PREPARATION** 10 minutes

125g/4¹/₂oz light Greek feta cheese, cubed

8 vine-ripened tomatoes, deseeded and cut into chunks

1 small cucumber, cut into chunks

100g/3¹/₂oz black olives

2 tbsp lemon juice

1 tsp dried oregano

freshly ground black pepper

1 Arrange the feta, tomatoes, cucumber and olives on a plate.

2 Spoon the lemon juice over the salad. Scatter with the oregano and season with plenty of black pepper. Leave the salad for up to 2 hours before serving, so it is at room temperature.

Health Benefits
Reduced-fat dairy products contain slightly more calcium than their regular counterparts , which is good for the bones and teeth and is thought to have a positive effect on blood pressure.

Food Facts per Portion

Calories 122kcal • Total Fat 7.7g • saturated fat 3.4g

Desserts

Following a low-fat diet doesn't mean that you have to avoid desserts altogether, as this chapter reveals with its tempting collection of recipes, ranging from Chocolate & Brandy Creams to Apricot Syllabub.

Much is made of fresh fruit, which is, of course, naturally low in fat and also packed with nutrients. Choose from Mango with Lime, Pineapple & Ginger Crush, Mango Sorbet and Pear Strudels. There are also reduced-fat versions of favourites that are usually high in fat, such Banana & Strawberry Yogurt Ice, Peach Crumbles/Crisps, Indian Rice Pudding and Mango Fool.

Low-fat dairy products make indulgent desserts while keeping fat levels down: simply replacing 200ml/7fl oz/scant 1 cup full-fat milk with the same quantity of semi-skimmed milk cuts the amount of saturated fat by 2.9g and saves you 40 calories. To see how delicious desserts made with low-fat dairy products can be, try Red Berry Fool, which uses ricotta (a naturally low-fat cheese) and low-fat yogurt.

Finally, whipped egg whites can make a rich and creamy dessert with scarcely any fat. Just try the Chocolate Orange Mousse and the Meringues with Strawberry Cream and you'll see what I mean!

Raspberry Sparkle

Not so much a dessert as a low-fat treat! You could serve the drink as an accompaniment to a platter of fresh fruit as part of a dinner-party dessert.

SERVES 4   **PREPARATION** 5 minutes

20 raspberries

2 tsp golden caster/superfine sugar

700ml/22fl oz/2²/₃ cups chilled Prosecco

1   Put the raspberries in a bowl and crush lightly with the back of a spoon. Divide between four Champagne flutes.

2   Divide the sugar between the glasses and top up with the Prosecco before serving.

Health Benefits

Raspberries are little baubles of goodness that are best eaten raw, because cooking can deplete their rich vitamin C content. They are said to be effective in treating menstrual cramps and have detoxifying capabilities.

Food Facts per Portion

Calories 142kcal · Total Fat 0.1g · saturated fat 0g

Mango with Lime

Mango can be a bit fiddly to prepare, but it is well worth the effort. Just make sure the fruit is very ripe for the best flavour.

SERVES 4   **PREPARATION** 15 minutes

---

2 ripe mangoes

juice of ½ lime

few fine strips of lime zest

4 scoops mango sorbet (see page 214), to serve (optional)

1   Put one of the mangoes on a chopping board and slice in half lengthways on either side of the stone, also cutting away any remaining flesh. Use a sharp knife to slice each half in a criss-cross pattern down to the skin. Repeat with the other mango.

2   Holding each mango half skin-side down, press it inside out, then cut the mango cubes away from the skin and put them in a serving bowl with the flesh from the stone and any juices.

3   Squeeze the lime juice over the mango and sprinkle with lime zest. Serve with a scoop of mango sorbet, if liked.

Health Benefits
Bursting with the antioxidants vitamin C and beta carotene, mango also provides the minerals calcium, magnesium and potassium.

Food Facts per Portion
Calories 117kcal • Total Fat 0.2g • saturated fat 0.1g

Minted Papaya & Melon

This is a simple dessert that makes a refreshing finish to a spicy meal, such as curry. Mint, fresh papaya and melon are natural partners, with the summery herb enhancing the flavour of the fruit. Make sure the fruit is ripe to ensure the best flavour.

SERVES 4 **PREPARATION** 10 minutes

1 large, ripe papaya

300g/10½oz peeled watermelon, cut into cubes

4 tbsp fresh orange juice

4 fresh mint sprigs, leaves only

1 Peel the papaya using a vegetable peeler, then cut in half and scoop out and discard the black seeds. Cut the fruit into cubes.

2 Put the papaya, watermelon and orange juice in a serving bowl and scatter over the mint before serving.

Health Benefits

Papaya contains an enzyme called papain, which aids digestion, while mint is similarly good for the digestive system, making this an excellent dessert after a heavy meal. The skin, hair and nails all benefit from the high levels of vitamin C and beta carotene.

Food Facts per Portion

Calories 42kcal • Total Fat 0.3g • saturated fat 0.1g

Pineapple & Ginger Crush

Ginger and pineapple are delicious together and make a refreshing granita that is especially good after a spicy meal.

SERVES 4   **PREPARATION** 30 minutes, plus freezing

400g/14oz peeled and cored fresh pineapple, cut into cubes

2.5cm/1in piece fresh root ginger, peeled and grated

4 pieces crystallized ginger, finely chopped

2 tbsp clear honey

1   Finely chop the pineapple in a food processor (you don't want it too smooth or puréed).

2   Mix together the pineapple with both types of ginger and the honey until combined. Transfer the mixture to a freezer-proof container and freeze for about 2 hours or until semi-frozen.

3   Mix to break up the ice crystals just before serving. Serve in chilled tall glasses.

Health Benefits

Pineapple, like papaya, contains an enzyme called papain, which is a digestive aid. It also has antibacterial and anti-inflammatory properties due to the presence of bromelain. Studies show that it may improve circulation in people with narrowed arteries.

Food Facts per Portion

Calories 80kcal • Total Fat 0.2g • saturated fat 0g

Fruit Bowl

The melon in this easy-to-prepare dessert is transformed into a serving bowl in which the fruit salad is arranged.

SERVES 4   **PREPARATION** 10 minutes

½ large Charentais or Cantaloupe melon

selection of fresh fruit, such as raspberries, strawberries, cherries, grapes, nectarines or kiwi, prepared and cut into bite-sized pieces

2 tsp lemon juice

1 Cut a sliver off the base of the melon half to give it a steady base, then stand it on a serving plate. Remove the seeds and discard, then, using a melon baller or spoon, scoop out most of the flesh to leave a hollow bowl shape.

2 In a bowl, mix together the prepared fruit with the melon balls and any juice. Add the lemon juice and turn to coat the fruit. Spoon the prepared fruit into the melon 'bowl' and serve.

Health Benefits

Fresh fruit is one of nature's top convenience foods: nutritious, low in fat, requiring little or no preparation, versatile and low in calories. People who eat generous amounts of fruit (and vegetables) on a daily basis, as part of a healthy diet, tend to have a reduced risk of chronic diseases, such as some forms of cancer, heart disease and type 2 diabetes, compared to people who eat only small amounts.

Food Facts per Portion

Calories 90kcal • Total Fat 0.4g • saturated fat 0.1g

Orange Granita

This couldn't be easier to make, and for a special treat you could grate over some good-quality plain chocolate just before serving.

SERVES 4   **PREPARATION** 30 minutes

juice of 4 freshly squeezed oranges

2 tbsp lemon juice

fine strips of orange zest (preferably unwaxed)

1   Pour the orange juice into a shallow freezer-proof container and stir in the lemon juice until combined.

2   Freeze the juice for 1 hour, then beat it with a wooden spoon. Repeat this process at 40-minute intervals over a 4-hour period to break the crystals down into small icy chunks.

3   Spoon the granita into four glasses and sprinkle with the orange zest before serving.

Storage
Can be stored for up to 3 months in the freezer.

Health Benefits
Lemons are rich in vitamin C, which can reduce the severity and length of colds and flu, and helps the body to absorb iron from foods.

Food Facts per Portion
Calories 20kcal • Total Fat 0g • saturated fat 0g

Mango Sorbet

This zingy sorbet makes a refreshing finish to a meal.
Alternatively, if you serve it in a wafer cone, it makes a healthy
summery snack.

SERVES 6–8

PREPARATION 35 minutes, plus freezing   **COOKING** 5 minutes

120g/4¼oz/½ cup golden caster/superfine sugar

2 large ripe mangoes

juice of 3 freshly squeezed oranges

1 egg white

1   Put the sugar and 300ml/10½fl oz/1¼ cups water in a saucepan
and stir over a medium heat until the sugar has dissolved.
Bring the mixture to the boil, then reduce the heat and
simmer for 5 minutes. Remove from the heat and leave to cool.

2   Prepare the mangoes following the instructions on p.209.
Put the mango flesh, orange juice and sugar syrup in a food
processor or blender and process until the fruit is puréed.

3   Pour the mixture into a freezer-proof container and freeze for
2 hours until semi-frozen. Remove from the freezer and
transfer to a bowl. Break up any ice crystals using a hand
whisk or fork.

4 Whisk the egg white in a grease-free bowl until it forms stiff peaks, then, using a metal spoon, fold it into the semi-frozen mixture. Return the mixture to the freezer-proof container and freeze until solid.

5 Remove from the freezer about 30 minutes before serving to allow to soften.

Storage

Can be stored for up to 3 months in the freezer.

Health Benefits

Oranges are known for their high vitamin C content, the highest amount of which is in the juice. This antioxidant plays a vital role in the body, disarming free radicals and preventing cell damage.

Food Facts per Portion

Calories 147kcal · Total Fat 0g · saturated fat 0g

Banana & Strawberry Yogurt Ice

Lower in fat than cream-based ices, yogurt produces a slightly tangy end result but is still rich and creamy. It is important to whisk the ice occasionally during freezing to give a smooth texture.

SERVES 6–8 **PREPARATION** 30 minutes, plus freezing

450g/1lb/4 cups strawberries, halved if large

2 ripe bananas, sliced

225g/8oz/1 cup 0% fat Greek yogurt

225g/8oz/1 cup 2% fat Greek yogurt

4 tbsp icing sugar/confectioner's sugar, or to taste

1 tsp vanilla extract

1 Purée the strawberries and bananas in a food processor or blender. Add the yogurts, icing sugar/confectioner's sugar and vanilla extract and process briefly until combined. Taste and add a little more icing sugar/confectioner's sugar, if necessary. Pour into a freezer-proof container. (This creamy mixture can also be eaten in its pre-frozen form.)

2 Freeze the mixture for 2 hours, then remove from the freezer and whisk to break up any ice crystals. Smooth into an even layer, then return to the freezer for another 2 hours. Repeat the whisking process to break up the ice crystals, then smooth out and return to the freezer again until solid.

3   Remove from the freezer 30 minutes before serving to allow
to soften.

Storage
Can be stored for up to 3 months in the freezer.

Health Benefits
Bananas are excellent sources of potassium, which is an important
mineral for the health of the heart and maintaining normal blood
pressure. They are high in carbohydrates, therefore good for
boosting flagging energy levels, and low in fat.

Food Facts per Portion
Calories 129kcal • Total Fat 0.9g • saturated fat 0.5g

Griddled Nectarines with Vanilla Cream

Fruit is delicious cooked in a griddle pan, as it becomes slightly caramelized. Use nectarines that are only just ripe rather than too soft, as otherwise they will become mushy in the pan.

SERVES 4	PREPARATION 15 minutes	COOKING 3–5 minutes

2 tbsp fresh orange juice

4 just-ripe nectarines, pitted and thickly sliced

Vanilla cream:

4 tbsp quark

½ tsp vanilla extract

1 tbsp icing sugar/confectioner's sugar

1   Put the orange juice in a bowl and add the nectarine slices; turn until the fruit is coated in the juice.

2   Heat a griddle pan over a high heat. Remove the nectarine slices from the juice and put them in the griddle pan. Cook for 3–5 minutes, turning once, or until slightly caramelized.

3   Meanwhile, in a bowl, beat together the quark, vanilla extract and icing sugar/confectioner's sugar to make the vanilla cream.

4   Arrange the nectarine slices in shallow bowls and pour over any juices left in the pan. Serve with a spoonful of the vanilla cream.

Storage

The nectarines can be stored in an airtight container in the refrigerator for up to 1 day, then served cold. The vanilla cream can be stored in the same way for up to 3 days.

Health Benefits

Much of a nectarine's vitamin C content lies just under the skin, so it is best to eat the fruit unpeeled. Nectarines are also an excellent source of beta carotene, which is converted into vitamin A in the body and plays a role in reducing the risk of heart problems and some forms of cancer.

Food Facts per Portion

Calories 76kcal • Total Fat 0.1g • saturated fat 0g

Raspberry Creams

Ⓥ 🍃 🥚 🌿 🐟

Indulgent and low in fat in equal measure, this creamy fruit dessert makes the most of calcium-rich 0% fat Greek yogurt, which has all the taste and creaminess but none of the fat found in regular equivalents.

SERVES 4   **PREPARATION** 10 minutes   **COOKING** 3 minutes

2 tbsp sunflower seeds

400g/14oz/1¾ cups 0% fat Greek yogurt

1 tsp vanilla extract

3 tbsp toasted wheat germ

225g/8oz/1⅓ cups raspberries

4 tsp maple syrup

1 Put the sunflower seeds in a frying pan and dry-fry over a medium-low heat for 2–3 minutes until light golden in colour, shaking the pan occasionally. Take care because they can burn easily.

2 In a bowl, mix together the yogurt, vanilla extract and wheat germ. Gently fold the raspberries into the yogurt and stir to give a marbled effect.

3 Spoon the creamy mixture into four glasses, top with the toasted seeds and drizzle with the maple syrup before serving.

Storage

The dessert can be prepared up to a day in advance, but scatter the sunflower seeds over the top only just before serving in order to retain their crunchy texture.

Health Benefits

Wheat germ, the heart of the wheat kernel, is a good source of protein, polyunsaturated fat, fibre, vitamins and minerals. It's the most nutritionally dense part of the wheat kernel and has been found to reduce LDL (harmful cholesterol) in the body – this has been attributed to the presence of the antioxidant vitamin E.

Food Facts per Portion

Calories 152kcal • Total Fat 4.7g • saturated fat 0.7g

Mango Fool

Ripe mango is so juicy and sweet that very little extra sugar is needed to make this deliciously creamy dessert. Chilling the fool before serving allows it to set. As an alternative to the mango, you could use fresh or frozen strawberries for an equally delicious result.

SERVES 4　　　　**PREPARATION** 15 minutes, plus chilling

2 ripe mangoes

200ml/7fl oz/generous ¾ cup reduced-fat fresh custard

4 tbsp 0% fat Greek yogurt

2 egg whites

1 Prepare the mangoes following the instructions on p.209. Put the mango flesh in a food processor or blender and purée until smooth. Press the mixture through a sieve into a bowl to remove any fibres, then stir the custard and yogurt into the mango purée.

2 Whisk the egg whites in a grease-free bowl until they form stiff peaks. Using a metal spoon, fold the egg whites into the mango (adding a spoonful at first, then folding in all the remainder) and turn until incorporated into the mixture.

3 Spoon the mixture into four glasses and chill for about 1 hour before serving.

Storage

Can be stored in an airtight container in the refrigerator for up to 1 day.

Health Benefits

Dairy products are an important source of calcium, magnesium and phosphorus, which are essential for healthy bones and teeth. They also contain significant amounts of B vitamins and zinc. However, make sure you opt for low-fat dairy products.

Food Facts per Portion

Calories 96kcal • Total Fat 0.3g • saturated fat 0.2g

Red Berry Fool

This pretty pink dessert can be eaten straightaway if you're in a hurry, but it does benefit from being chilled for 30 minutes, if time allows, so it can set. It is also good made with fresh or frozen strawberries.

SERVES 4   **PREPARATION** 15 minutes, plus chilling

200g/7oz/scant 1 cup ricotta cheese

1–2 tbsp clear honey, to taste

300ml/10½fl oz/1¼ cups 1% fat vanilla bio yogurt

400g/14oz/scant 2½ cups raspberries, hulled

1   Put the ricotta in a food processor or blender and blend until smooth. Next, add 1 tablespoon of the honey and the vanilla yogurt and blend the mixture until smooth and creamy; taste for sweetness and add more honey, if necessary.

2   Reserving 4 of the raspberries, put the remainder in a bowl and crush them lightly with the back of a fork. Fold them into the creamy mixture to give a rippled effect. Spoon the raspberry fool into four glasses, then chill for 30 minutes. Decorate with the reserved raspberries before serving.

Storage

Can be stored in an airtight container in the refrigerator for up to 1 day.

Health Benefits

Although honey provides little in the way of nutrients, it does have medicinal and healing properties. It is an effective antiseptic and can help to bring relief to sore throats, diarrhoea and asthma.

Food Facts per Portion

Calories 155kcal • Total Fat 6g • saturated fat 3.6g

Variations

Mango, peach, nectarine or plum can all be used instead of the raspberries. They are best puréed until smooth, then stirred into the yogurt and ricotta mixture to give a rippled effect.

Apricot Syllabub

This is not an everyday pudding but one that makes a special-occasion treat. It is important to use apricots at their peak of ripeness when making this dessert; the best ones are sunshine-gold in colour and full of juice.

SERVES 4   **PREPARATION** 20 minutes   **COOKING** 10 minutes

250g/9oz ripe apricots, halved, pitted and sliced

100ml/3½fl oz/scant ½ cup dry white wine

80ml/2½fl oz/⅓ cup half-fat extra-thick double cream

2 egg whites

55g/2oz/¼ cup fructose

1   Put the apricots and wine in a saucepan and bring to the boil, then reduce the heat and simmer, half-covered, for 8 minutes until the apricots have softened and the wine has reduced. Leave to cool, then put in a blender or food processor and purée until smooth.

2   Whip the cream until it forms soft peaks, then fold in the apricot purée.

3   Whisk the egg whites in a grease-free bowl until they form stiff peaks. Whisk the fructose into the egg whites.

4   Using a metal spoon, gently and gradually fold the egg white mixture into the cream and apricot purée. Spoon the syllabub into four small glasses and chill for 1 hour until set.

Storage

Can be stored in an airtight container in the refrigerator for up to
1 day.

Health Benefits

Apricots are a valuable source of fibre as well as beta carotene, an
antioxidant with both heart and eye-protecting capabilities.

Food Facts per Portion

Calories 131kcal · Total Fat 3.5g · saturated fat 2.2g

Variations

Peaches and nectarines can be used instead of the apricots. Peel
them first by immersing them in just-boiled water for a couple of
minutes, which should make the skins easier to remove.

Soufflé Berry Omelette

Light, fluffy and delicious, this sweet omelette is packed with juicy berries. Use fresh berries if in season, although frozen ones are also good and, conveniently, are sold in different fruity combinations as well as singly.

SERVES 2   **PREPARATION** 10 minutes   **COOKING** 3 minutes

2 eggs, separated

1 tsp icing sugar/confectioner's sugar

2 tsp sunflower oil

100g/3½oz/1 cup frozen mixed berries, defrosted

1   Beat the egg yolks in a large mixing bowl. Whisk the egg whites in a grease-free bowl until they form stiff peaks, then whisk in the icing sugar/confectioner's sugar. Using a metal spoon, carefully fold the egg whites into the egg yolks.

2   Heat a medium, non-stick frying pan. Add the oil and, using a crumpled piece of kitchen towel, wipe oil over the base of the pan. Spoon in the frothy egg mixture and flatten it with a spatula to cover the base, then cook for 1 minute.

3   Spoon the berries down the centre of the omelette and cook for another 2 minutes or until the bottom of the omelette is set and golden. Fold the omelette in half to encase the berries and slide it on to a plate; cut it in half to serve.

Health Benefits

Purple berries such a blackberries and blueberries are rich in beneficial anthocyanin pigments and bioflavonoids, which act as antioxidants, inhibiting the growth of cancer cells and protecting against cell damage by carcinogens. Blackberries also give us vitamins C and E, which work together in the body, and are also effective antioxidants. The fruit is just as good frozen as fresh.

Food Facts per Portion

Calories 121kcal • Total Fat 8.7g • saturated fat 2g

Chocolate & Brandy Creams

Chocolate, brandy and orange make indulgent partners, yet this dessert belies the complex flavours with its simplicity of preparation. Serve this rich, mousse-like dessert chilled, if time allows.

SERVES 4   **PREPARATION** 10 minutes, plus chilling

125g/4^{1}/$_2$oz/scant ^{2}/$_3$ cup ricotta cheese

350g/12oz/1 cup virtually fat-free fromage frais

4 tbsp brandy

2 tbsp icing sugar/confectioner's sugar, or to taste

125ml/4fl oz/^{1}/$_2$ cup fresh orange juice

2 tsp finely grated orange zest

40g/^{1}/$_2$oz plain chocolate, 70% cocoa solids, finely grated

fine strips of orange zest, to decorate

1   Beat together the ricotta, fromage frais, brandy, icing sugar/ confectioner's sugar, orange juice and zest in a bowl. Taste and add a little more icing sugar/confectioner's sugar, if necessary.

2   Spoon half of the ricotta mixture into four glasses and top with half of the chocolate.

3   Spoon the remaining ricotta mixture into the glasses and sprinkle with the rest of the chocolate. Chill for 1 hour, then decorate with the orange zest before serving.

Storage

Can be stored in an airtight container in the refrigerator for up to 2 days.

Health Benefits

Plain chocolate contains bioflavonoids, a powerful antioxidant that appears to protect the arteries by preventing the formation of plaque. Studies show that plain chocolate can reduce blood pressure and improve blood flow. It also has a low glycaemic index, helping you to reduce spikes in blood-sugar levels.

Food Facts per Portion

Calories 202kcal • Total Fat 6.3g • saturated fat 3.9g

Chocolate Orange Mousse

V O

You can't beat a rich chocolate dessert, but even a low-fat one should be regarded as an occasional treat only – sorry!

SERVES 4   **PREPARATION** 25 minutes, plus chilling

70g/2½oz good-quality plain chocolate, at least 70% cocoa solids

juice of 1 freshly squeezed large orange

finely grated zest of 2 oranges

2 eggs, separated

1   Melt the chocolate in a heatproof bowl set over a pan of gently simmering water, making sure the bottom of the bowl does not touch the water. Leave to cool, then beat in the orange juice, zest (reserving a little to sprinkle) and egg yolks.

2   Whisk the egg whites in a grease-free bowl until they form stiff peaks. Using a metal spoon, gently fold a large spoonful of the egg whites into the chocolate mixture, then fold in the rest until combined.

3   Spoon the chocolate mixture into four small cups (espresso ones are fine) or ramekins, then chill until set. Sprinkle with the remaining orange zest before serving.

Storage

Can be stored in an airtight container in the refrigerator for up to 2 days.

Health Benefits

Good news for egg lovers: the British Heart Foundation has changed its advice, confirming that eating more than the recommended 4 eggs a week will not raise cholesterol levels in the body. It is now suggested that proteins in eggs can be converted into enzymes that improve blood flow and blood pressure.

Food Facts per Portion

Calories 133kcal • Total Fat 7.7g • saturated fat 3.7g

Peach Crumbles/Crisps

Traditionally, crumble/crisp is high in fat, but this low-fat version comes with a crisp oaty cinnamon topping. Serve with a spoonful of low-fat custard.

SERVES 4 　　　　**PREPARATION** 15 minutes 　　　　**COOKING** 15–20 minutes

4 tbsp whole porridge oats

2 tbsp sunflower seeds

½ tsp ground cinnamon

1 tbsp fructose

4 just-ripe peaches, halved and pitted

1 Preheat the oven to 180°C/350°F/Gas 4. Mix together the oats, sunflower seeds, cinnamon and fructose. Sprinkle the mixture over the top of each peach half.

2 Arrange the peaches in an ovenproof dish. Pour 2 tablespoons water into the dish to prevent the fruit becoming too dry. Bake in the preheated oven for 15–20 minutes or until the topping is slightly crisp and the fruit is tender.

Storage

The crumble/crisp mixture can be stored in an airtight container for up to 5 days.

Health Benefits

They may look unassuming, but sunflower seeds contain valuable amounts of vitamin E, which improves circulation and enhances the immune system. They also contain omega-6 fatty acids, which has been found to reduce harmful cholesterol levels.

Food Facts per Portion

Calories 136kcal • Total Fat 4.7g • saturated fat 0.5g

Pear Strudels

Filo/phyllo pastry is deliciously crisp and golden when baked, and is lower in fat than many other types of pasty, particularly puff. Here it is used in a quick and simple-to-make tart.

SERVES 4   **PREPARATION** 20 minutes   **COOKING** 20 minutes

8 filo/phyllo pastry sheets

40g/1¹/₂oz/3 tbsp half-fat butter, melted

2 ripe, but not mushy, pears, peeled, halved and cored

1 tbsp lemon juice

1 tsp ground cinnamon

4 tsp clear honey

1   Preheat the oven to 200°C/400°F/Gas 6. Take one sheet of pastry and lightly brush one half with some of the melted butter. Fold in half and brush again. Put another sheet on top, lightly brush one half with the butter and fold over – you should have an 18 x 15cm/7 x 6in rectangle.

2   Put a pear half in the centre of the filo/phyllo rectangle and brush over a little lemon juice, then sprinkle with a quarter of the cinnamon. Gather the pastry up around the pear and scrunch it up to make a small tart. Put on a baking sheet lined with parchment paper.

3   Repeat to make 3 more pear strudels. Bake in the preheated oven for 20 minutes until golden. Remove from the oven and leave to cool slightly, then drizzle with the honey before serving.

Health Benefits

Rich in pectin and soluble fibre, pears are valuable in that they have the ability to keep us regular as well as reducing levels of harmful cholesterol in the body – welcome news for those people suffering with atherosclerosis. Despite their high water content, pears are a good source of vitamin C.

Food Facts per Portion

Calories 106kcal • Total Fat 5g • saturated fat 1.2g

Indian Rice Pudding

This creamy rice pudding is flavoured with aromatic cardamom, saffron and nutmeg. It is made on the hob rather than baked in the oven, so is much quicker to cook.

SERVES 4   **PREPARATION** 10 minutes   **COOKING** 35–40 minutes

150g/5$^{1}/_{2}$oz/$^{3}/_{4}$ cup brown short-grain rice, rinsed

600ml/21fl oz/scant 2$^{1}/_{2}$ cups 1% fat milk

4 cardamom pods, bruised

$^{1}/_{2}$ tsp freshly grated nutmeg, plus extra to serve

pinch of saffron threads

2 tbsp golden caster/superfine sugar

2 tbsp clear honey

1 tbsp toasted flaked almonds

1 Put the rice in a heavy-based saucepan and cover with 500ml/17fl oz/2 cups boiling water. Bring to the boil and cook, uncovered, for 15 minutes.

2 Pour the milk into the pan, then add the cardamom, nutmeg, saffron and sugar. Reduce the heat and simmer, partially covered, for 20–25 minutes, stirring regularly, or until the rice is tender.

3 Spoon the rice into four bowls, grate over a little more nutmeg, drizzle with the honey and top with the almonds.

Storage

The rice pudding can be stored in an airtight container in the refrigerator for up to 3 days and served cold.

Health Benefits

Unlike white rice, brown rice is unrefined and therefore retains most of its fibre and nutrients, such as vitamins B and E. Almonds are a good source of vitamin E, which benefits the heart. They are low in saturated fat and contribute omega-3 fatty acids as well as fibre, which aids their cholesterol-lowering properties.

Food Facts per Portion

Calories 269kcal • Total Fat 3.6g • saturated fat 0.8g

Apricot & Brazil Nut Bars

Ⓥ Ⓞ Ⓐ Ⓖ

These nutritious, granola-type bars are packed with energy-giving dried fruit, nuts and seeds. Serve as a simple dessert with low-fat yogurt or include in a packed lunch.

MAKES 10

PREPARATION 20 minutes, plus chilling   **COOKING** 3 minutes

50g/2oz/$\frac{1}{3}$ cup Brazil nuts, roughly chopped

50g/2oz/$\frac{1}{2}$ cup whole porridge oats

2 tbsp pumpkin seeds

2 tbsp sunflower seeds

100g/3$\frac{1}{2}$oz/$\frac{2}{3}$ cup raisins

150g/5$\frac{1}{2}$oz/scant $\frac{3}{4}$ cup ready-to-eat dried apricots, cut into small pieces

4 tbsp fresh orange juice

1   Line a 25 x 18cm/10 x 7in baking tin with rice paper.

2   Put the nuts and oats in a frying pan and dry-fry over a medium heat for 3 minutes, turning them occasionally, until they begin to turn golden and the oats become crisp. Remove from the pan and leave to cool.

3   Put the nuts, oats and seeds in a food processor and process until very finely chopped. Tip the mixture into a mixing bowl.

4   Put the raisins, apricots and orange juice in the food processor and process until they form a smooth, thick paste. Scrape the fruit mixture into the mixing bowl with the nuts and seeds and stir well until combined.

5   Tip the fruit and nut mixture into the prepared tin and, using a palette knife, smooth into an even layer, about 1cm/½in thick. Chill in the refrigerator for 1 hour before cutting into 10 bars.

Storage

Can be stored in an airtight container for up to 5 days.

Health Benefits

Brazil nuts are one of the richest sources of selenium – an essential mineral that can protect the body against cell damage, which can lead to cancer. It is also a known mood enhancer, and eating just 3 Brazil nuts a day will provide the recommended daily amount. Like other nuts, Brazils contain monounsaturated fat, which has been found to benefit the cardiovascular system.

Food Facts per Portion

Calories 141kcal • Total Fat 6.8g • saturated fat 1.3g

Meringues with Strawberry Cream

Ⓥ Ⓞ ⓪

Yes, meringues are low in fat, but they are also high in sugar, so it's best not to indulge on a too regular basis. For a special treat, serve with this strawberry compote and thick Greek yogurt – low-fat, of course!

MAKES 10   **PREPARATION** 15 minutes   **COOKING** 1 hour 10 minutes

4 egg whites

300g/10$\frac{1}{2}$oz/1$\frac{1}{3}$ cups caster/superfine sugar

2 tsp white wine vinegar

2 tsp cornflour

500g/1lb 2oz/4$\frac{1}{2}$ cups strawberries, hulled,
   10 reserved for decorating

300g/10$\frac{1}{2}$oz/generous 1$\frac{1}{4}$ cups 0% fat Greek yogurt

2 tbsp icing sugar/confectioner's sugar

1 tsp vanilla extract

1   Preheat the oven to 180°C/350°F/Gas 4. Line 2 baking sheets with parchment paper and draw 5 x 8cm/3$\frac{1}{2}$in circles on each sheet. Turn the sheets over.

2   Using an electric hand mixer, whisk the eggs whites in a grease-free bowl until they form stiff peaks. Gradually whisk in the sugar until the mixture is shiny and stiff, then whisk in the vinegar and cornflour.

3 Spoon the mixture onto the circles on the parchment paper and make dips in the centre of each one with the back of a spoon.

4 Bake in the preheated oven for 10 minutes, then reduce the oven to 120°C/250°F/Gas ½ and cook for 1 hour. Remove the meringues from the oven and leave to cool a little before transferring to a wire rack.

5 Purée the strawberries in a blender or by pressing them through a sieve. (If using a blender, you may wish to press the purée through a sieve afterwards anyway to remove any seeds.)

6 Beat together the yogurt, icing sugar/confectioner's sugar and vanilla extract in a bowl. Spoon the mixture into the dips in the meringues and spoon over the strawberry purée. Finally, decorate with the reserved strawberries.

Storage

The meringues can be stored in an airtight container for up to 5 days.

Health Benefits

Strawberries can protect the skin against ageing thanks to a combination of bioflavonoids and vitamin C. These protect against the appearance of thread veins and wrinkles, and also help to heal blemishes and bruises.

Food Facts per Portion

Calories 158kcal • Total Fat 0.1g • saturated fat 0g

Menu plans

Nut-free 5-day menu

Allergies to nuts and seeds are becoming increasingly common, and, as the symptoms can be life-threatening, it is essential to take every precaution to avoid contact with nuts, seeds and by-products. Always check food labels.

Day 1
BREAKFAST: Winter Fruit Compote, 0.7g total fat (see page 18)
LUNCH: Warm Chicken Salad with Avocado Dressing, 9g total fat (see page 80)
DINNER: Poached Eggs with Spiced Chickpeas, 10.9g total fat (see page 184)

Day 2
BREAKFAST: Char-grilled Chicken & Pepper Toasts, 4.2g total fat (see page 34)
LUNCH: Cajun Salmon Roll, 14.4g total fat (see page 88)
DINNER: Pork & Vegetable Ramen, 11.9g total fat (see page 128)

Day 3
BREAKFAST: Strawberry & Ricotta Muffins, 3.6g total fat (see page 18)
LUNCH: Chilli Beef Fajitas, 6.9g total fat (see page 64)
DINNER: Provençal Prawns/Shrimp, 5.3g total fat (see page 182)

Day 4
BREAKFAST: Soufflé Tuna Omelette, 7.6g total fat (see page 42)
LUNCH: Mexican-style Turkey Burgers, 10.8g total fat (see page 86)
DINNER: Mixed Bean & Vegetable Tagine, 3.4g total fat (see page 196)

Day 5
BREAKFAST: Kedgeree, 6.6g total fat (see page 38)
LUNCH: Gazpacho with Avocado Salsa, 6.4g total fat (see page 108)
DINNER: Beef & Mushroom Stir-fry, 9.3g total fat (see page 132)

Vegetarian 5-day menu

This menu is designed to provide all the nutrients required when following a low-fat vegetarian diet, which is free from meat, poultry, seafood and all animal-derived foods.

Day 1
BREAKFAST: Strawberry & Ricotta Muffins, 3.6g total fat see page 18)
LUNCH: Spring Vegetable Couscous, 6.9g total fat (see page 114)
DINNER: Lentil & Vegetable Dahl, 3.8g total fat (see page 204)

Day 2
BREAKFAST: Boiled Egg with Asparagus, 7g total fat (see page 52)
LUNCH: Mediterranean Tortilla Parcel, 7.2g total fat (see page 116)
DINNER: Spring Vegetable Stir-fry with Cashew Nuts, total fat 12.8g
  (see page 190)

Day 3
BREAKFAST: Fruit & Nut Muesli, 21.5g total fat (see page 24)
LUNCH: Tofu & Miso Soup, 2.8g total fat (see page 106)
DINNER: Mushroom & Spinach Open Lasagne, 11.1g total fat
  (see page 194)

Day 4
BREAKFAST: Avocado & Black Olive Toasts, 10.4g total fat (see page 48)
LUNCH: Eggs Florentine, 9.1g total fat (see page 118)
DINNER: Vegetable Goulash, 4.1g total fat (see page 198)

Day 5
BREAKFAST: Banana Porridge/Oatmeal, 9.2g total fat (see page 26)
LUNCH: Provencal Pizza, 3.9g total fat (see page 120)
DINNER: Poached Eggs with Spiced Chickpeas, 10.9g total fat
  (see page 184)

Vegan 5-day menu

This menu avoids any foods derived from animals, including meat,
fish, poultry, eggs, dairy and honey. In some cases, recipes have
been adapted to suit a vegan diet; use soya, rice or oat milk, yogurt
and cheese, if appropriate, although please bear in mind that these
could alter the fat content.

Day 1
BREAKFAST: Almond Banana Shake, 11.9g total fat (see page 17)
LUNCH: Tofu & Miso Soup, 2.8g total fat (see page 106)
DINNER: Mixed Bean & Vegetable Tagine, 3.4g total fat (see page 196)

Day 2
BREAKFAST: Avocado & Black Olive Toasts, 10.9g total fat (see page 48)
– use vegan mayonnaise
LUNCH: Spicy Cauliflower Salad, 7.6g total fat (see page 110) – serve with
vegan pâté instead of the egg
DINNER: Thai Green Vegetable Curry, 8.1g total fat (see page 202)

Day 3
BREAKFAST: Fruit & Nut Muesli using low-fat vegan yogurt and soya milk,
21.5g total fat (see page 24)
LUNCH: Gazpacho with Avocado Salsa, 6.4g total fat (see page 108)
DINNER: Spring Vegetable Stir-fry with Cashew Nuts, 12.8g total fat
(see page 190)

Day 4
BREAKFAST: Winter Fruit Compote using dairy-free cream, 0.7g total fat
(see page 20)
LUNCH: Provencal Pizza, 3.9g total fat (see page 120)
DINNER: Lentil & Vegetable Dahl, 3.8g total fat (see page 204)

Day 5
BREAKFAST: Griddled Tomatoes on Toast, 3.1g total fat (see page 46)
LUNCH: Japanese-style Smoked Tofu Salad, 8.3g total fat (see page 112)
DINNER: Bean, Fennel & Red Bell Pepper Salad, 3.9g total fat
(see page 186)

Wheat- & gluten-free 5-day menu

For people allergic or intolerant to wheat and gluten, this menu is easy to follow, balanced and also low in saturated fat. It may be necessary to monitor your intake of carbohydrate foods, especially if diabetic, and this menu will allow you to do this. Please note that adapting some of the recipes to suit a wheat- and gluten-free diet may have altered their fat content.

Day 1
BREAKFAST: Berry Scrunch, 9.9g total fat (see page 19)
LUNCH: Warm Chicken & Lentil Salad, 5.8g total fat (see page 76)
DINNER: Pork with Minty Pea Purée, 8.7g total fat (see page 126)

Day 2
BREAKFAST: Smoked Trout Rolls, 4.3g total fat (see page 37) – serve with gluten-/wheat-free bread
LUNCH: Spicy Cauliflower Salad, 7.0g total fat (see page 110)
DINNER: Coriander Chicken with Lemon Quinoa, 7.9g total fat (see page 142)

Day 3
BREAKFAST: Mozzarella & Tomato Stacks, 10.9g total fat (see page 44)
LUNCH: Pea & Bacon Soup, 4.5g total fat (see page 57)
DINNER: Spring Vegetable Stir-fry with Cashew Nuts using tamari, 12.8g total fat (see page 190) – serve with brown rice

Day 4
BREAKFAST: Fresh fruit Compote with Yogurt, 4.9 total fat (see page 22)
LUNCH: Ricotta & Herb Pate, 6.6g total fat (see page 104) – serve with wheat-/gluten-free bread
DINNER: Vietnamese Beef Broth using tamari, 5.3g total fat (see page 130) – serve with wheat-/gluten-free noodles

Day 5
BREAKFAST: Breakfast Frittata, 8.4g total fat (see page 32)
LUNCH: Pasta (wheat/gluten-free) with Lamb & Rocket, 10g total fat (see page 60)
DINNER: Halibut with Tomato, Red Onion Relish, 3.8g total fat (see page 168) – serve with mashed potato

Index